GUIZHOU

The author dedicates this book to Dui Jian Feng who traveled with me to most regions of Guizhou and enthusiastically collected information on every aspect of life in the province. Without him the book could not have been written.

Acknowledgments

I would like to thank all my friends in Guizhou Province who have been so generous with their time and expertise in helping me with this book. In particular: Yang Shengming, Tourism Administration of Guizhou Province; Tang Ru Xiang, Guizhou Overseas Travel Corporation; the guides and staff of Guizhou Overseas Travel Corporation and CITS, especially Dui Jian Feng, Lu Chang (Annie), Zhang Peng Hua and Zhu Gui Hua; Yang Ai Hua, Foreign Affairs Bureau, Liupanshui City; the professors and lecturers of the Guizhou Institute For Nationalities, Guiyang, especially Li Ting Gui, Gu Puguang, Pan Ding Zhi and Pan Chao-Lin; Wang Peishan of Guizhou Institute of Biology; Liang Wei, Guizhou Provincial Tourism Bureau; Luo Zailin, Guizhou Local Chronicles Association; Cheng Jingping, Industrial Arts Research Institute; Ma Zhengrong, Chinese Artists Association; Yang Hua, Taijiang Miao Embroidery Handicraft Workshop; Siu-Woo Cheung, Anthropology Department, University of Washington; Jane Hancock, my secretary.

Gina Corrigan was born and educated in the UK and holds a BSc in geography from London University and a Masters of Education from Nottingham University. She is co-author of a geography text book on China (Heinemann Educational Press, 1982) and has co-produced over 20 educational film strips on China and Europe for Gateway Audio Visual Publications with her husband, Peter.

GUIZHOU

— ✺ —

Text and Photography by
Gina Corrigan

PASSPORT BOOKS
a division of *NTC Publishing Group*
Lincolnwood, Illinois USA

Published by Passport Books in conjunction with
The Guidebook Company Ltd

This edition first published in 1995 by Passport Books, a division of NTC Publishing Group, 4255 W.
Touhy Avenue, Lincolnwood (Chicago), Illinois 60646-1975 USA.
Originally published by The Guidebook Company Ltd © The Guidebook Company Ltd. All rights
reserved.

ISBN: 0-8442-9896-4
Library of Congress Catalog Card Number: 94-67163

Grateful acknowledgment is made to the following authors and publishers for permissions granted:

Hamish Hamilton Ltd and Aitken, Stone & Wylie Ltd for
Riding the Iron Rooster by Paul Theroux © 1988 by Cape Cod Scriveners Co

Bantam Books Inc, a division of Bantam Doubleday Dell Publishing Group Inc for
Living Treasures by Tang Xiyang © 1987 by Bantam Books Inc and The New World Press

MacMillans Publishers Ltd and Harper & Row for
The Long March by Harrison E Salisbury © 1985 by Harrison E Salisbury

The Nationality Press, Beijing, for
Clothings and Ornaments of China's Miao People © 1985

Fu Jen Catholic University Press Ltd, Taipei, for
Miao Textile Design © 1993 by Fu Jen Catholic University Press Ltd

Weidenfeld & Nicholson Ltd for
Peking by Anthony Grey © 1988 by James Murray Literary Enterprises Ltd

Editor: Carey Vail
Series Editor: Anna Claridge
Illustrations Editor: Caroline Robertson and John Oliver
Design: De•Style Studio
Map Design: Tom Le Bas and Bai Yiliang

Front cover: Gina Corrigan; back cover: collection Carey Vail
Additional illustrations courtesy of: The Parsons Collection, Museum of Mankind, Trustees of the British
Museum, London 36, 126, 240–241; Hong Kong China Tourism Photo Library 58–59, 100, 119, 123,
165; paper cuts, collection Eric Boudot 75, 94; Hanart T Z Gallery 112; Walter Gardiner Photography
168; collection Gina Corrigan, Abbas Nazari, James Hockey Gallery 170, 171, 172 (above), 173, 174;
line drawings by Sidney Clark 190, 191, 192

Production House: Twin Age Limited, Hong Kong
Printed in Hong Kong by Sing Cheong Printing Co Ltd

*Miao girl at Langde village wearing the traditional silver crown and
jewellery of festivals and weddings*

Contents

Terraced rice fields near Huangguoshu at harvest time

Introduction

Guizhou, one of China's lesser known provinces and best kept secrets, opened to tourists in the late 1980s. This is one of the most beautiful provinces, offering dramatic karst limestone scenery, a spectacular plateau landscape cut by great gorges and canyons, terraced hillsides and enchanting vistas. The many attractions include waterfalls, untouched forests alive with rare species of plants and animals, underground cave complexes and caverns with superb displays of stalactites and stalagmites resembling great fluted cascading curtains. Here are some of the most superb examples in Asia, offering tremendous potential for hikers, potholers and nature lovers.

Guizhou is a multicultural province with the fifth largest ethnic population in China. Thirteen distinct ethnic groups live alongside Han Chinese who have migrated there from all regions of the country. The variety of ethnic groups living in Guizhou make up 34 per cent of the total population of 32 million. A major charm of the province for travellers is the number of festivals, resplendent with colour and suffused with music, that take place throughout the year and that remain an important part of continuing traditional lifestyles and customs.

Guizhou is situated in southwest China and is bordered by Yunnan to the west, Sichuan to the north, Hunan to the east and Guangxi to the south. It lies between latitude 24.3° and 29° north with a total area of 176,100 square kilometres (67,992 square miles), or 1.8 per cent of the total area of China. Eighty-seven per cent of the province is mountainous (above 500 metres, 1,640 feet), ten per cent hilly (200–500 metres, 656–1,640 feet) and the remaining three per cent a flat plain. Its magnificent mountain scenery has earned Guizhou the nickname 'province of parks'.

Guizhou is located on the eastern slope of the Yunnan-Guizhou Plateau which decreases in height from northwest to southeast. It is part of two major river basins, the Chang Jiang (Yangzi River) and the Xi Jiang (Pearl River). The Miaoling mountain area in central Guizhou is the watershed. The Wu Jiang and its tributaries flow north into the Chang Jiang connecting Guizhou with Sichuan Province to the north. Rivers in the south, such as the Beipan and Nanpan, are tributaries of the Hongshui He River which becomes the Xi Jiang in the lower reaches.

The Wumeng and Dalou mountain area in the north of the province, the highest in Guizhou, run southwest to northeast and rise to 2,900 metres (9,500 feet). To the southeast of these mountains is a dissected limestone plateau with an average height of 1,000 metres (3,280 feet), rising in some areas to 2,500 metres (8,200 feet) and falling to 200–500 metres (656–1,640 feet) in the valleys.

Guizhou is officially made up of 86 county units—59 counties, 12 autonomous counties, four special districts, six towns under local administrations and five urban districts. For the convenience of travellers, this guide organizes Guizhou into five main regions; central, southeast, southwest, northeast and northwest.

History

Stone Age artefacts have been found in at least 20 of Guizhou's counties, attesting to its rich history. The earliest written records date from the Shang Dynasty (c. 16th–11th century BC) when Guizhou was referred to as Guifan. However, its exact area and borders are very uncertain. By the Western Zhou Dynasty (11th century–771 BC), Guizhou was known as Zhang Ke and was inhabited by various ethnic peoples living in tribal groupings. It was not part of the Chinese Empire at that time. This period is sometimes called the Bai Yue (Hundred Minorities) period. The inhabitants belonged to the Dai linguistic group that includes the Shui, Dong, Bouyei and Zhuang. They were characterized by the use of a bronze drum played at important ceremonies. Later, people belonging to the Tibeto-Burman group arrived from the west. These included the Yi, Naxi and Tujia. The Miao came from the north and east. Zhang Ke and a second state centring on Anshun came into economic contact with the well-established Han Chinese states to the north. In the strong Han Dynasty (206 BC–220 AD) and in the Three Kingdoms period (220–265 AD) forces were sent to conquer the region. This was only marginally successful, and the area continued to be ruled by local tribal chiefs. However, local grave finds, like the Han-style bronze horse and chariot found at Xingyi in 1975, on display in Guiyang Museum, indicate the presence of rich Han Chinese living in the region.

Throughout the Tang period (618–907), the Han Chinese exerted authority in the area, which they considered part of the Chinese Empire, sending in troops to control it when necessary. To retain autonomy, tribal chiefs of the various ethnic groups living in Guizhou gave tribute to the Han Empire. During the Song Dynasty (960–1279), some regions fell under Han administration while others remained autonomous. The Yuan Dynasty (1271–1368) marked a major change in policy when Chinese military forces collected taxes directly from local tribal chiefs who exerted power over their own clans. There were no civil governors representing the Han Empire during this period.

By the time the Ming (1368–1644) came to power, central control was more heavily exercised over the Guizhou region. Guizhou had become a province of China with a governor in control. Local clan heads collected taxes that were often paid in specialities of the area such as horses. Tribal chiefs belonging to the numerous ethnic groups were pressurized by the Han to give up their powers but it was a slow process. During the Ming period, pressure was exerted by establishing military garrisons and

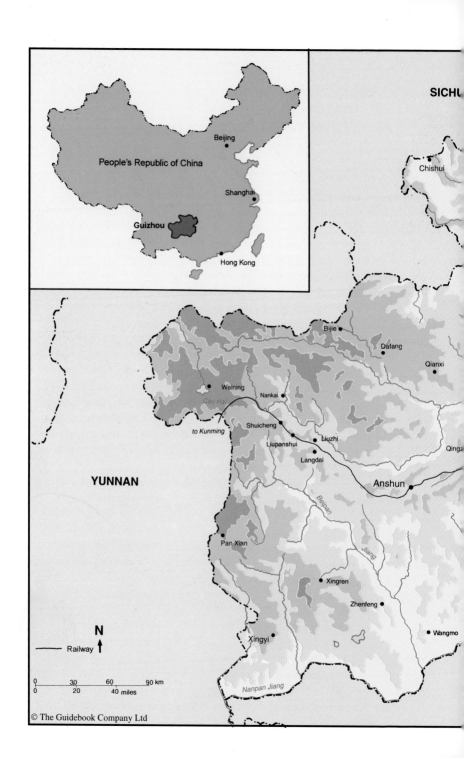

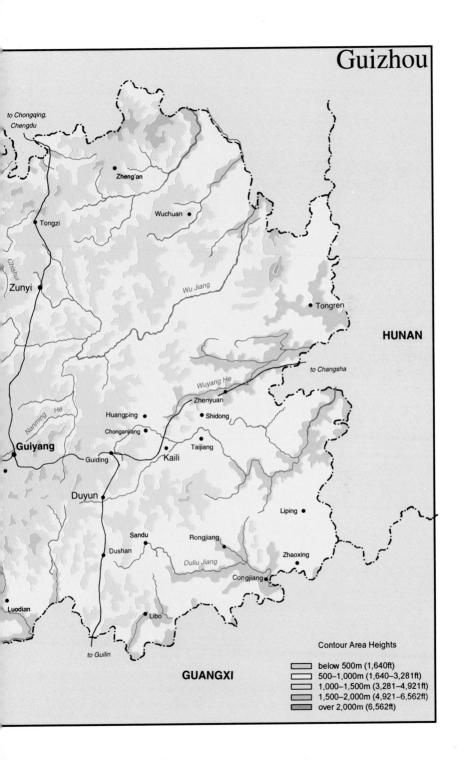

Guizhou

to Chongqing,
Chengdu

Zheng'an

Wuchuan

Tongzi

Chishui

Zunyi

Wu Jiang

Tongren

HUNAN

Nanming He

to Changsha

Wuyang He

Zhenyuan

Huangping   Shidong

Chonganjiang

Guiyang   Taijiang

Guiding   **Kaili**

Duyun

Liping

Sandu   Rongjiang

Dushan   Zhaoxing

Duliu Jiang

Congjiang

Luodian

Libo

to Guilin

GUANGXI

Contour Area Heights

	below 500m (1,640ft)
	500–1,000m (1,640–3,281ft)
	1,000–1,500m (3,281–4,921ft)
	1,500–2,000m (4,921–6,562ft)
	over 2,000m (6,562ft)

Guizhou was frequently a staging post for troops while the Ming launched attacks on rebellious border areas such as Yunnan. Soldiers often farmed and colonized the land as well as putting down local uprisings. Wives often followed the army and families stayed on to farm after military service had been completed. Other Han Chinese, looking for new opportunities in trade and business, followed the army, along with Han peasants hungry for new land. In this way a number of Han people set up permanent homes and farms in Guizhou.

There were many uprisings in Guizhou against the Han Chinese, led notably by the Miao with the help of other tribal groups. Ethnic groups wanted their freedom and autonomy, resenting interference from outside. In the 16th century, a particularly bloody battle was led by the tribal chief Yang Yin Long, a Yi. The Ming central government had to send in troops from four Chinese provinces to put down the uprising, which lasted for 27 months in the Bozhou area, near Zunyi. The Han Chinese defeated the tribal groups and Central Government in Beijing set up a firm administration under their own bureaucrats to govern and gather taxes. The Han Chinese established schools and Confucian ethics became more common.

By the middle of the 17th century the borders of Guizhou were almost the same as today. The ethnic groups, often joined by local Han, never surrendered completely to Han Chinese rule. There were thousands of uprisings, which persisted into and through the Qing Dynasty (1644–1911), largely because taxes were heavy and agricultural production low due to poor weather and difficult physical conditions.

Relative stability came with the setting up of the People's Republic of China in 1949. Landlords were overthrown and the land was redistributed to the peasantry, who had already been educated in the new Socialist values by the Red Army during its march through northern Guizhou towards Yanan. Since 1949, autonomous prefectures and counties have been set up to give the various ethnic groups some power over their own affairs.

Geography

The area supports a wide range of plant life from subtropical to temperate due to the well-defined vertical distribution from the valley floors, lying at approximately 200–500 metres (656–1,640 feet), to heights of 2,900 metres (9,500 feet).

The soils, largely formed from limestone, contain impurities such as quartz and clay. The valley floors are the richest areas while the hillside soil is shallow and rocky, making farming difficult. The valley slopes have been cut out and are planted with rice and, as the terraces become increasingly steep and the land stony and arid, with maize. The ingenuity used in constructing these man-made staircases is spellbinding. Above cultivation level is forest or scrub. Many of these areas are covered with azaleas and rhododendrons that look particularly beautiful when they flower in the spring.

The table below confirms the difficult farming conditions and the high percentage of wasteland and forest.

LAND USE	PERCENTAGE
Cultivated land	10.5
Forest	12.6
Pasture	24.3
Water surface	1.5
Urban and Wasteland	51.1

Almost all crops ranging from those of the subtropical to the warm temperate zones are grown in Guizhou and there are thick forests of fir and pine as well as lush broad-leaved forest.

Commercially, 'Jingping 18-year fir' is the most important for its timber while other commercial trees include the lacquer tree that is used to produce fine Dafang lacquer products. (**Warning**: Contact with the lacquer tree can cause severe allergy in some people.) Tung oil is made from the nuts of the tung tree; camphor wood is also produced commercially outside Zunyi. Rare trees, protected by the government, are of interest to botanists and include the silver yew, dove tree, Taiwan yew, and *spinulosa* tree fern.

Guizhou, with its many rare species of plants and animals, offers a tremendous amount to botanists, notably in the Fanjing and Jinshagou nature reserves.

Agriculture

Eighty-two per cent of the population live in rural areas. Guizhou is one of the poorest regions of China because of its thin limestone soil. Land reforms, beginning in 1949 (see page 18), have been replaced gradually since 1978 with new liberal initiatives and the 'Family Responsibility System' that has improved the life of the peasant farmer. Larger agricultural surpluses and a wider variety of goods are now produced. These are sold at the 'free markets', which are a regular feature of the Chinese countryside, usually a half-day's walk from peasants' homes. Public transport or tractors are also used to transport produce to the markets. The variety and quality of vegetables, herbs, fruit, fish, meat and eggs have improved a hundredfold, but the prices in these markets are much higher than in State shops; urban workers with fixed salaries find food expensive. However, as everywhere in China, food has always been considered one of the most important items of expenditure.

The relative wealth resulting from recent agricultural changes has allowed for improvements to housing, such as replacing the traditional thatched or bark roofs with tiles, an increase in housing construction, and the revival of large funerals and weddings.

State education in rational land use, covering new crops and technology, as well as new market demands, has led to increased yields and specialized farming. South Guizhou, a traditional grain-producing area, now supplies the capital, Guiyang, with a wide range of fruit and vegetables year-round. Other areas specialize in cash crops such as tobacco, sugar-cane and rape for oil. The Miao in particular, along with other ethnic groups, live mainly in the many poor mountain areas of the province, where each family pays a minimal rent for the use of the land, rather than fulfilling a quota. This system has been designed to encourage production and investment. One Miao village, 30 kilometres (18.6 miles) from Guiyang, now supplies the urban area with fruit including peaches, apples and pears.

Urban migration, however is on the increase. Male family members in particular are moving to the cities for work as many peasant families are large and the family land is too small to divide.

Duck farming near Anshun

CROPS

Since the 6th century AD, **rice** has been the most important staple in China. Paddy rice was first grown in southwest China and later, with the development of irrigation, in the north. In Guizhou, rice is grown on the floor of the valleys and on the lower terraces where irrigation is possible.

Planting rice seedlings

Rice seed is sown into nursery fields in March and transplanted by hand into the paddy fields at the end of April or early May. In some parts of southeast Guizhou, seedlings are grown indoors and then transplanted out by hand into a nursery bed. The plants are placed 3.8 centimetres (1.5 inches) apart. Four weeks later, when the seedlings have grown to 15–20 centimetres (6–8 inches), they are transplanted to the paddy fields. Six to eight seedlings are planted 15 centimetres (6 inches) apart in clumps so that when fully grown they can be harvested by one stroke of the sickle. Paddy fields are kept flooded throughout the growing season as rice 'likes its feet in the water and head in the sun'. Harvesting is done by hand in September or October, depending on the variety, during the dry season. It is dried in stooks, then threshed and stored with the husk on. The irregularly-shaped fields are usually ploughed by water buffalo or, in some areas, by oxen, who also provide manure and do not have to be 'fed' with valuable petrol. In autumn, the land is either left fallow or, more commonly, **rape** is sown to clean the fields, provide an important cash crop and supply animal fodder. Rape is harvested in April and the field ploughed and harrowed in preparation for rice transplantation.

In the past, the Miao generally favoured **glutinous rice** but as this requires more irrigation, various species of high-yield, short-stemmed rice have been introduced. Generally only one crop of rice, the main staple, is grown in Guizhou. There are 30 varieties of grain. Particularly famous is a black rice called 'black pearl', found in Huishui County.

Winter **wheat** is common in the valleys and on terraced hillsides and is followed by rice in the lowlands, maize on the hillsides. Summer wheat is sometimes grown and interplanted with cotton, a cash crop. Wheat is grown for flour that is made into noodles, eaten at breakfast or dinner.

LAND REFORM 1949–1994

The formation of the People's Republic of China in 1949 heralded a period of major and dramatic agrarian reform. Land held by landlords was gradually turned over to the peasantry who were so poor, however, that they did not have the resources to improve it. The Chinese Communist Party encouraged families to work together in mutual aid teams of 6–15 households sharing tools and labour. From 1953 larger units were instigated, often called Elementary Production Co-operatives (EPC), comprising 30–40 households. Land use and resources under each EPC were controlled by management committees. Peasants still owned their land, animals and tools for which they received rent or hire payment. The EPC retained a proportion of the total harvest for investment purposes and the rest was divided equally between each household. Small plots near the house, known as 'private plots', were worked by the peasants for their own vegetables, pigs and chicken.

From 1955, Advanced Production Co-operatives (APC) of 100–300 families were formed and ownership of the land was transferred to the co-operatives. Larger items such as draught animals were purchased from the peasants. The management committees, usually formed of Party cadres, had little or no experience of running such large units and consequently production decreased. Peasants resented the loss of their newly-won land. Some cadres went on to abolish private plots and banned traditional activities such as basket-making, pig rearing and weaving that had provided extra income for the peasants. Eventually, because pig manure was recognized as an essential by-product for maintaining land fertility, the Party relented and peasants were again allowed to keep pigs in styes near their houses. Private plots for cultivating vegetables were also reinstated.

The government, however, continued its policy of collectivization and in 1958, the year of the Great Leap Forward, People's Communes were initiated by amalgamating APCs. By the end of 1958, 750,000 APCs had been combined into 26,000 communes throughout China. Guizhou Province was no exception to these developments. The aim of each commune, made up of 4–5,000 households, was to be self-sufficient. It was administered by Party and Revolutionary committees that interpreted Central Government policy and, in turn, made recommendations to Central Government. Below this level the commune was divided into brigades, similarly run by committees, that set up small industries. Finally, each brigade was divided into teams, which usually comprised a village, although large villages were often subdivided. The team was the basic accounting unit. It received production quotas from the brigade while its various committees organized the ploughing, sowing and harvesting of crops. Peasants were paid according to the amount of work they did and the amount earned by the team once the crop was sold to the State. Money had to be put aside for tax, welfare, production costs and a reserve fund that established small workshops in the villages. Peasants usually retained private plots for their own needs. Irrigation and road schemes were administered by the commune for which peasants could be called out to work at any time in mass mobilization campaigns. One major aim between 1959 and 1976 was to increase production of grain, often at the expense of other crops. The independently-minded peasants did not approve of the communes. They often did minimum work and production did not rise significantly despite the increased use of chemical fertilisers and the introduction of improved varieties of cereals. Official statistics showing huge production figures were usually falsified. Little could be changed until Mao Ze Dong died in 1976.

From then, Central Government, under Deng Xiao Ping's leadership, formulated new policies. It wanted to stimulate economic activity and agricultural production as well as increase the range of agricultural products. The commune system was now seen as inefficient; from 1978 communes were broken up and a new 'Family Responsibility System' gradually took over. Land was redistributed to individual families or households who were given a quota to fulfil and were paid accordingly. Any goods produced over and above the quota received a better price. Families could opt to sell these goods at free markets where they could command even higher prices. The quota system became more flexible and was not, as previously, always in grain. The quota for families living outside the city was usually in fruit and vegetables while, if the land was better suited to pasture, the quota was in animal produce. This allowed peasants to return to growing what most suited their land. The old commune was completely abandoned and a new administrative area, called a 'township', replaced it. This is often bounded by the area of the old commune and is run by a management committee that receives the required quota levels from Central Government and informs each family production unit of its commitments.

Other staples are grown in the mountainous areas of Guizhou. **Millet** is one of the oldest crops grown in China. It is the most drought-resistant of all cereals, easy to harvest, thresh and store as it has a hard outer shell, and its nutritional content is high with nine per cent protein. The straw is a useful forage for livestock. **Sorghum**, cultivated for thousands of years, is sometimes grown for food in the mountains as it is also drought-resistant. In the north, sorghum is grown for the production of **Maotai**, the firey Chinese liquor.

The Miao also grow **maize** as a staple. Maize was introduced to China in the 16th century. In the uplands it is grown on narrow terraces carved into the hillside and is often intercropped with sweet potato, soy beans or squash, which help to stabilize the soil and provide green manure. The advantage of maize is that it needs less water than rice or wheat. In areas with better transport and sufficient land, maize is grown industrially, from which cornstarch and fructose syrup are manufactured. The stems are often used for paper manufacture while the grain is used as fodder for chickens, ducks, pigs and cattle. **Barley** is used as forage and for brewing. **Buckwheat** is grown in the very remote, poor mountainous areas of northwest Guizhou.

Sweet potato, which came to China via the Silk Road, is resilient to environmental stress and is grown extensively being a good staple that can be stored successfully and used industrially, while the green tops are a particularly good pig food when boiled. It is usually dried, stored and then eaten fried and is a good reserve if the main staples are destroyed by flooding, hence its name locally, the 'golden potato'. The **Irish potato** came to China in the 17th century and is grown in Guizhou mainly as a vegetable. It is planted in the spring and is beneficial to the mountain communities for its high calorific value, mineral-rich content and easy storage ability. Like the sweet potato it is sliced, dried and stored. It is commonly eaten baked by the ethnic groups or sliced and cooked in a sauce by the Han Chinese. It is also an important animal food.

Life has always been a struggle for survival in the mountain areas where, in the past, even **bracken roots** were eaten by the Miao of northwest Guizhou. Roots were collected, pounded with wooden mallets and then steeped in water in large wooden tubs for two to three days. A brown starch left at the bottom was dried and then steamed with maize meal.

Soy bean, grown in China for 5,000 years, is a major food crop with a high nutritional value of 40 per cent protein and 20 per cent oil. Originally from northern China, the soy bean was brought south with Chinese settlers and is grown by ethnic people in the valleys and on the lower hillsides. It is eaten as bean curd, heavily spiced with red chillies. Some mountain communities cannot grow soy bean but it is available from markets in numerous forms. It is grown intercropped with maize or planted after early rice. One advantage of soy bean is that it fixes nitrogen in the soil

Glutinous rice drying

from the atmosphere through bacteria found in the root nodules. It has been introduced to many of the ethnic groups throughout the province because of its use as a biofertiliser. Surpluses can be sold for industrial use as the oil can be used to make, among other commoditites, high-grade resin paint, pharmaceutical products and synthetic rubber.

CASH CROPS

A wide variety of **vegetables** are grown as cash crops, including tomatoes, onions, cabbages, mushrooms, aubergines (eggplant), gourds, kohlrabi, taro, beans and bean shoots. Broad beans, introduced to China along the Silk Road, are an important spring cash crop used for noodles. Great importance is put on fresh vegetables which are traded at the market with an equally wide range of **herbs** including ginger and chillies.

Encircling each town and city is a belt of market gardens. The new demand for **fruit** from higher-income city dwellers is being met by an expansion of peach, pear, apple and cherry orchards, as well as citrus fruits such as tangerines in the south. Guiyang even offers strawberries. Lichees, loquats and water melons grow in the south and you can find excellent persimmons and Chinese gooseberries, known in the West as kiwi fruit, in central Guizhou.

Cash crops have increased with the new market economy and with the abandonment of State policy that required rice to be grown by each family. **Tobacco** and rape are perhaps the most important. **Rape**, introduced from the West along the Silk Road, is advantageous to the farmer since it can be planted in the autumn and harvested in the spring before the rice is planted. The growing season is short and it is adapted to cold temperatures. Rapeseed oil is one of the main cooking oils and is used in industry for soaps and paints. **Sugar cane**, one of China's most ancient crops, is grown in southern Guizhou and is manufactured into sugar. Demand for this is growing with the increase of confectionery in a wealthier society. **Cotton** is not a large cash crop as the weather is too wet. **Tea** is also a significant crop.

ANIMAL HUSBANDRY

Most families keep their own chickens, pigs and draught animals. Surplus is sold in the free markets. Beef has never been a popular meat in China but cattle can be raised on mountain pastures and production has been encouraged recently. Grasslands in the uplands are extensive and many of the poor areas are being reseeded with the help of experts from New Zealand and Australia to improve the nutritional value for sheep and beef stock. Sheep are kept largely for their wool in the northwest of the province and there are flocks of goat. Goat meat is popular among the ethnic groups. Dog is reared for meat and a number of villages specialize in 'dish dog'.

Beehives are kept in many places in the countryside, especially in the spring and summer. Some families specialize in honey production and bees are trucked out to good locations where they can feed. Honey is extracted by workers who live in tents on the site. When the flowers die the hives are moved to more favourable locations. Honey is exported but is also enjoyed by the Miao who eat it on glutinous rice and by town dwellers who buy it especially for their children for its health-giving properties.

Industry

Guizhou was considered a poor inland province in 1949. It was economically undeveloped without a manufacturing base. The people were largely uneducated and there was a high incidence of disease such as malaria, leprosy, smallpox and syphilis. Opium smoking was rampant. The province was controlled by warlords and communication was limited due to the mountainous terrain, thereby cutting it off from the coast and the Treaty Ports that were the major areas of industrial development. Mao Ze Dong's policy in the 1950s was to move industry inland and to the provincial capitals so that it was dispersed and less vulnerable to attack. Skilled Chinese with a zeal to spread Socialism volunteered to take up jobs in undeveloped areas. Many came to Guizhou to help develop a modern infrastructure and industry. Railways were built to link Guizhou with other provinces and gradually it became less isolated.

RAILROAD	DISTANCE	COMPLETED
Guiyang–Liuzhou (Guangxi)	607 km (377 miles)	1944
(renovated after 1949)		
Guiyang–Chongqing (Sichuan)	463 km (288 miles)	1965
Guiyang–Kunming (Yunnan)	637 km (396 miles)	1966
Guiyang–Zhuzhou (Hunan)	902 km (560 miles)	1972

Guizhou's many raw materials have formed the basis for industrial development. Over 74 different minerals and 26 metals have been found in the province. The most important mineral is mercury; Guizhou has the largest reserves in China. Other raw materials include silicon, used in the production of chemical fertilisers, optical crystal, iodine, calcite, clay and bauxite. The bauxite is particularly rich in aluminium and silica but has a low ferric content and has the advantage of being easy to mine. Phosphorous ores, again the largest reserves in China, are also of a high quality. Coal reserves are the fourth largest in China with a wide range of type. Guizhou is often referred to as 'the sea of coal in southwest China'. Iron ore reserves are substantial. There are also timber reserves. Because of the numerous rivers, steep falls and high rainfall, Guizhou has a huge potential for hydroelectric power, its capacity being the sixth largest in China.

Today, industry is developing in the cities of Guizhou, led by large industrial bases in Guiyang and Anshun. Eighteen per cent of the population now live in the cities. Guizhou remains largely a primary producer of agricultural products and minerals, but industry will undoubtedly become increasingly important in its economic development.

For Love of the Railway

I woke to find myself in the rocky province of Guizhou, all pyramidal limestone hills and granite cliffs. The landscape was green and stony, like Ireland, and the people lived in rugged Irish-looking stone cottages, and houses with rough-hewn beams. They were the strongest houses I saw in China, and around them, marking the limits of their land, were beautifully built drystone walls, symmetrical and square.

Among these great slanting slab-like hills there was very little arable land, and not many flat places for farming. The gardens were made by balancing walls and building terraces, and by all the other useful things that could be made from the chunks of stone—bridges, aqueducts, roads, dykes and dams. The villages were thick with villas and two-storey houses (it was rare in the country to find more than one floor), all of them stone-built, with slate roofs. And their grave-mounds were just as solid and built with the same granite confidence: the cemeteries were miniature versions of the villages.

While the honeymooners nipped down to the dining-car for the breakfast of rice gruel and noodles, I ate some bananas I had bought in Kunming and drank my green tea. We passed Anshun ('once the centre of the opium trade') and we stopped a while at Guiyang, where I met Mr Shuang.

Mr Shuang was in his late sixties, plum-faced and whiskery, with a shapeless cap and a red armband that showed he was a railway worker. But he was a retired man who out of boredom had gone back to be a platform supervisor.

'I was sick of staying at home,' he said. 'I've been doing this job for half a year. I like it. But I don't need the money.'

He said he earned 130 yuan a month.

'What do you spend it on?'

'I don't have children or a family, so I buy music.' He smiled and said, 'I love music. I play the harmonica.'

'Do you buy Chinese or western music?'

'Both. But I like western very much.'

'What kind?'

He said in a neatly enunciating way, 'Light orchestral music.'

That was the kind that was played in the train and in the railway stations when they weren't playing Chinese songs. They played 'The Skaters' Waltz' and 'Flower Of Malaya' and selections from Carmen.

'Do you get many travellers in Guiyang?'

'Unfortunately, very few people come here. This province was closed to foreigners until 1982. Some people pass through but they don't stop. And yet we have many places to see—some very nice temples, and the Huangguoshu Falls and the hot springs. Please come back to Guiyang and I'll show you around.'

It seemed that the more remote and countrified the place in China, the more hospitable the people were.

For the onward journey the honeymooners had changed their clothes: he wore a jacket and sun-glasses, she wore a tweed skirt. They smoked and slumbered. Maybe this fatigue meant it was the end of their honeymoon?

By mid afternoon we were in the south-east of Guizhou, among greener hills showing the scars and broken terraces of having once been farmed. The route to Guilin was roundabout, because of all the mountains. They were an obstruction, but they were very pretty—velvety and shaggy with grass and trees. It was much hotter now, and most of the train passengers were asleep, barely stirring at Duyun; that place looked like Mexico, with a big yellow-stucco station and palm trees under a clear blue sky.

Farther south the landscape changed dramatically: the grey hills here were shaped like camel humps, and chimney-stacks, and stupas with sheer sides. They were the oddest hills in the world, and the most Chinese, because these are the hills that are depicted in every Chinese scroll. It is almost a sacred landscape—it is certainly an emblematic one.

Paul Theroux, Riding the Iron Rooster, 1988

Getting There and Getting Around

Guizhou has always been considered very remote and difficult to get to as there has been no well-developed transport system. Historically, Han Chinese penetrated southeast Guizhou by following the tributaries of the Chang Jiang (Yangzi) southward into Guizhou. Consequently the most developed area is the southeast and here we find a strong Han culture. Because of its mountainous terrain, there were only trackways until the 1950s when the new government began to build roads to connect Guizhou with the other provinces of China. However, roads remain narrow with only room for two vehicles, except for the motorway between Guiyang, Anshun and Huangguoshu. Railways came late to Guizhou, not being built until the 1950s and 1960s. Travelling to and around Guizhou today is comparatively easy with improved transport and air links.

Getting There

BY AIR

The best way to get to Guizhou to begin a tour of the province is by air. At the beginning of the 1990s, a direct air link with Hong Kong was inaugurated. Flights now operate between Hong Kong and Guiyang on Mondays and Fridays with Guizhou International Air Service Company. Flight days may change—the company is planning to add a Wednesday flight— so check with your agent. As this is a charter flight, the fare is non-refundable. It is best to book your flight one month in advance from agents in Hong Kong. Travel agents that book flights include China Star Travel, the China National Aviation Corporation and China Travel Service (CTS) (see Practical Information, page 236). Payment is in Hong Kong dollars or if booking from abroad, in US dollars. The cost of a one-way ticket is in the region of US$200.

Air China, the international carrier, flies to Beijing and you can book onward flights to most major cities through their offices abroad. Direct flights leave for Guiyang from Guangzhou, Shanghai, Kunming, Chengdu, Guilin, Xi'an and Beijing—flights can be booked through airline offices in these cities or from agents in Hong Kong (see Practical Information, page 236). Domestic flights are still difficult to book from abroad, however other international airlines, such as Cathay Pacific and British Airways, can book onward flights to destinations within China.

The best place to book airline seats when you are in China is at Overseas Travel Corporation (OTC) or CITS (China International Travel Service) offices. You can also find travel agents in de luxe hotels. The best way to book an air package is through a Hong Kong agent.

BY RAIL

A train journey to Guizhou is well worth the experience as you travel through such wonderful scenery and can get a real feel for the way of life in the countryside and the daily rhythm of the people. Rail connections to Guizhou are possible from most major cities of China. Recently, rail fares have increased enormously—a first class rail ticket is almost as expensive as going by air. You can buy various classes of ticket. There are 'hard' or 'soft' seats, the words being self-explanatory, sitting for the whole journey. There are also 'hard' sleepers where you can lie down, stacked in three-bunk beds in a carriage with many other passengers. A 'soft' sleeper is in a compartment shared by four people. Duvets and hot water are provided.

Meals can be obtained from the restaurant car on long journeys but, unless you speak Chinese, the staff usually fail to understand. You can nearly always buy food at the numerous stations and fellow passengers are very willing to help foreigners who may be experiencing difficulties with the language.

Tickets can be bought from tourist offices in the cities in China or at railway stations, but the latter is notoriously difficult. Tickets can also be obtained from CTS in Hong Kong. There is a daily train service between Hong Kong and Guangzhou:

KOWLOON TO GUANGZHOU		GUANGZHOU TO KOWLOON	
Train 96	07:50/10:30	Train 91	08:15/10:55
Train 98	08:35/11:15	Train 93	10:00/12:40
Train 92	12:25/15:05	Train 95	16:13/18:53
Train 94	14:10/16:50	Train 97	18:00/20:40

Low season fare: Adult HK$230 (US$30) Child HK$115 (US$15)
Peak season fare: Adult HK$270 (US$35) Child HK$135 (US$17.50)

You can take one piece of luggage on the train at a cost of HK$80 (US$10)—book this in on the concourse of Kowloon Station at CTS.

DAILY TRAIN SERVICES TO GUIYANG FROM CITIES IN CHINA

Guangzhou to Guiyang		
Train 52	Depart 16:00	Arrive 21:00 next day
Shanghai to Guiyang		
Train 151	Depart 11:25	Arrive 08:27 on third day
Kunming to Guiyang		
Train 324	Depart 19:55	Arrive 08:46 next day
Chengdu to Guiyang		
Train 81	Depart 14:02	Arrive 08:38 next day

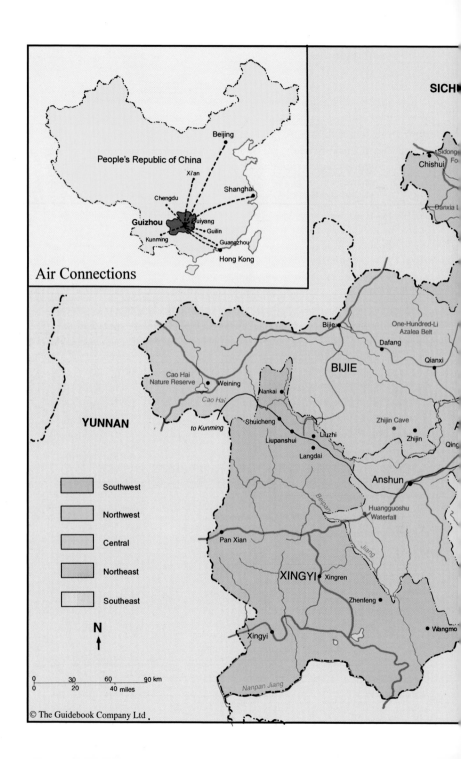

SICHU

People's Republic of China

Beijing

Xi'an

Chengdu

Shanghai

Guizhou Guiyang

Guilin

Kunming Guangzhou

Hong Kong

Air Connections

Sidong

Chishui

Fo

Danxia L

Bijie

One-Hundred-Li
Azalea Belt

Dafang

Qianxi

BIJIE

Cao Hai
Nature Reserve   Weining

Nankai

Cao Hai

YUNNAN

to Kunming   Shuicheng

Liupanshui

Langdai

Liuzhi

Zhijin Cave

Zhijin

Qing

Anshun

Huangguoshu
Waterfall

Southwest

Northwest

Central

Northeast

Southeast

Pan Xian

XINGYI   Xingren

Zhenfeng

Wangmo

N

Xingyi

Nanpan Jiang

| 0 | 30 | 60 | 90 km |
| 0 | 20 | 40 miles | |

© The Guidebook Company Ltd

By Road

Long-distance scheduled public buses run between towns, enabling you to travel to Guizhou by bus. You can buy tickets from the long-distance bus stations in the major cities of China. This is not easy unless you speak good Chinese.

Getting Around

Individual travel to most parts of the province is becoming increasingly easy, however, check first with GZOTC or CITS whether the areas to which you want to travel are open or closed as this alters from year to year. Unless you are prepared to walk into the countryside you are limited to the major bus routes between cities.

Reasonable standard hotels are available in the cities and in the countryside you can stay at Chinese-style guest houses, called *zhaodaisuo*, which means, 'a place to stay for a night simply'. These are of a varying standard and rooms usually do not have private facilities. If they do, they often do not work and you have to use public toilets which are of the squat kind, without privacy and generally not particularly clean. Prices vary. The price is more reasonable for Chinese nationals, slightly more expensive for overseas Chinese and vastly more expensive for other nationalities. Many hotels and guest houses have restaurants but generally food is better in the numerous privately-owned restaurants that now compete for business. You should ask advice from local people about the best places to eat. It is safe to eat at Chinese restaurants as long as you eat cooked food that has come straight from the stove to your plate. Even Chinese travellers carefully wipe bowls, glasses and chopsticks or use their own chopsticks. It is advisable to drink only boiled water or bottled drinks. Chinese beer is particularly good. All fruit should be washed and peeled.

Tours

To see the real beauty of Guizhou, it is worthwhile organizing an itinerary with a reputable agent or with Chinese friends. There are a few specialist tour operators in Hong Kong, Europe and America who organize tours in Guizhou. Information and details of various tours can be obtained from the Guizhou Overseas Travel Corporation (GZOTC) in Guiyang, China International Travel Service (CITS), or from Occidor Adventure Tours in the UK (see Practical Information, page 236).

By Road

Guizhou has a network of two-way tarmac roads between the major cities. These circuitous routes traverse mountains and valleys, making for long journeys between relatively short distances. There is a four-lane toll highway between Guiyang and

Anshun, continuing towards Huangguoshu Waterfall. This makes it possible to visit the waterfall, see Longgong (Dragon Palace) Cave and return to Guiyang in one day.

There is a long-distance bus service between major cities. You have to walk to the villages along small roads and pathways from the cities unless you are travelling with a tour group. Visitors tend to be taken to villages that are close to the road, but there are more remote villages over mountain paths that take several hours to walk to. Horses are not used a lot today and few jeeps are available for hire—the mountain tracks are often too narrow anyway.

On market days, hundreds of peasants will be walking to their nearest market, distances of between five and ten kilometres (three to six miles). Local people sometimes bicycle along the most difficult tracks but this is not advised unless you are an experienced mountain cyclist.

BUS SCHEDULES FROM GUIYANG

City	Distance		Bus Number	Departure
	Kilometres	Miles		
Anshun Huangguoshu	105	65	Special	Every half-hour
Longgong Huangguoshu	330	205	101	07:00
Waterfall	150	93	Regular	07:00
Longgong	137	85	Regular	07:00
Zhijin	157	98	137/139/259	07:20/08:00/08:40
Kaili	196	122	235	07:40
Zhenyuan	271	168	Regular	07:00
Shibing	240	149	233	08:20
Huangping	196	122	241	08:00
Tongren	466	290	205	07:20
Zunyi	163	101	221/223	10:00/11:00
Weining	342	213	Regular	07:00

By Rail

You can also travel by rail to the major towns within Guizhou and to nearby towns in surrounding provinces. Trains leave from Guiyang for Zunyi and Sichuan Province to the north; Kaili, Yuping and Hunan Province to the east; Anshun, Liuzhi and Shui-cheng to the west; and Duyun, Dushan and Guangxi Province to the south.

Tickets are available at railway stations or from local CITS agents. You are more likely to travel second class as it is difficult to get first-class rail tickets.

(following pages) *Miao Fertility Festival at Langde village, near Kaili*

Facts for the Traveller

Climate

Guizhou has a humid subtropical monsoon climate with relatively warm winters, mild summers and little seasonal contrast. It has a mean annual temperature of 15°–17°C (59°–63°F) and a mean annual precipitation of 850–1,600 milimetres (33.5–63 inches). There are an average of 270 frost-free days. Tremendous regional contrast occurs in both temperature and precipitation; the east tends to be wetter than the west. Guizhou is known for its local, distinctive climatic microcosms varying with altitude and aspect.

GUIYANG: MEAN MONTHLY TEMPERATURE AND RAINFALL

Jan	Feb	Mar	Apr	May	June	July	Aug	Sept	Oct	Nov	Dec	
2.8	5.6	11.7	17.2	21.7	22.2	24.4	25.0	20.0	13.9	11.7	8.3	°C
37	42	53	63	71	72	76	77	68	57	53	47	°F
25	28	23	74	178	209	229	104	138	107	51	15	mm
1.0	1.1	0.9	2.9	7.0	8.2	9.0	4.1	5.4	4.2	2.0	0.6	in

Total rainfall: 1,181 milimetres (46.4 inches). Altitude: 1,390 metres (4,560 feet)

Clothing

In Guiyang there are two international-standard hotels and here men will feel comfortable in a shirt, tie, trousers and sweater. Suits are worn for business. Women can wear their smarter clothing but there is no need for special evening clothes on holiday. Men and women dress casually in the city and certainly in the countryside. Women will feel comfortable in slacks, jeans or skirts and blouses with a sweater. You need a good pair of walking shoes or trainers to explore the countryside and villages. Since it rains in Guizhou in most seasons a plastic mac and umbrella are extremely useful. The summers are hot and sticky—cotton clothes are better than artificial fabrics. In spring and autumn, temperatures vary enormously from year to year so a range of clothing, a 'layered' approach, is required and an anorak is an important item. The temperature range is also enormous from one area to another because of the mountainous nature of the countryside.

Although Guizhou is in the subtropics, it can be very cool between November and April due to the high altitude. Be prepared with warm clothing and shoes. Snow is uncommon in most of Guizhou but it can fall in the northwest, while the rest of the province can feel quite bitter at times.

Many travellers will visit the ethnic people and stop at countryside fairs. To blend into the scene, wear plain simple clothing. Even then you will attract stares. Short skirts, shorts and low-cut tops will draw attention to yourself and people will make fun of you. Conservative dress in the streets is a good rule.

Packing

If you are touring with a group and staying only in Guiyang, you need not make any special preparations as most things are available in the city. However, it makes sense to bring items you might require so that you do not waste time looking for them. Take a small medical kit with useful items like Elastoplasts, antiseptic cream, insect repellent, a bandage, scissors, analgesics, lip salve, suncream, something to calm an upset stomach, throat lozenges, vitamin pills and a cold depressant, sterile needles and syringe pack. It is always a good idea to pack a course of antibiotics which suit you in case a cold changes to bronchitis. A dental repair kit is useful.

Bring all your toiletries although most things can be bought in the cities but not in the countryside. If you plan to explore the countryside, staying at small Chinese hotels and hostelleries, a cotton sleeping bag and towels are a good idea as these are not supplied. Extra toilet paper and paper handkerchiefs are useful.

Fruit is plentiful, whatever the season, and the Chinese-style food is usually excellent in the many restaurants, so you don't need to bring extra food unless you have a particular liking. Tea is readily available but if you like coffee, bring your own. Hot boiled water is provided in your hotel room. A penknife is a must to peel fruit with and wetwipes are useful to wipe your hands before meals. You can bring your own chopsticks, as many Chinese travellers do, to avoid possible hepatitis infection.

Make sure your suitcase has a good lock and use a strap. Luggage vans on trains will not accept suitcases without a lock. There is no laundry service except in the cities so bring travel wash and clothes that do not need ironing.

Travelling by air: make sure your suitcase does not exceed 20 kilograms (44 pounds) or you will be charged for the excess.

Photography

Colour print film is available in Guiyang but slide film is almost impossible to obtain, so bring all the film you need with you. Similarly, good quality batteries are difficult

Two Miao women early in the century, each with two babies wrapped in felt capes

to come by in Guizhou; bring your own. Take two cameras to be sure of getting the photographs you want—you will find it difficult to get any repairs done—and a zoom lens of 35–70 milimetres for good standard holiday photographs. Because the weather is so variable in Guizhou, it is wise to bring a range of film speeds from 64 to 200 ISO. Carry film in your hand luggage as X-ray machines for hold luggage may not be film safe.

Visas

All travellers to China must first get a visa. This can be obtained quite easily from your local Chinese embassy or consulate by submitting a completed visa application form with a passport-size photograph, your passport (valid for at least four months), a photocopy of your onward or return flight or proof of at least £600 (US$890) in traveller's cheques. The cost of an individual visa depends on your nationality; a British citizen currently pays £25 (US$37). In the UK, you can apply for a visa by post. For an application form, send a stamped addressed envelope to: The Visa Office, Consular Section, The Embassy of the People's Republic of China, 31 Portland Place, London, W1N 3AG.

Travel agents can often organize your visa for you. If you are travelling with a group, your travel agent will get a group visa which means you do not have to submit your passport. For business, work or student visas, apply to your nearest Chinese embassy or consulate for details.

A Chinese tourist visa is valid for a period of 90 days. Visa extensions can be obtained in China at the Public Security Bureau (Gong'an Ju) in most large cities but you must apply at least two days before the original visa expires. Your visa will allow you to travel to all major cities and areas open to foreigners. In Guizhou, some areas are closed to travellers. Check with the Public Security Bureau or tourist office to get an updated list. Closed areas change. At the time of writing, the areas around Bijie and Weining in northwest Guizhou, as well as some remote villages and country districts, are difficult to visit. Special permits can often be obtained once in China from local Foreign Affairs offices.

Customs And Immigration

Entering Guizhou: Whether you enter Guizhou by air to Guiyang or overland via Hong Kong–Guangzhou, customs and immigration is a fairly simple procedure. First, you hand in your Health Declaration form which assures the authorities that you have no known illness or symptom. Next, your passport is checked and stamped or your group visa is inspected. After retrieving your bag you will pass through customs. Customs declarations forms asking you to list how much money, jewellery, number of cameras, videos, washing machines and so on you are bringing with you have recently been abandoned. You are allowed to bring in four bottles of alcohol, three cartons of cigarettes, unlimited film and personal medical requirements. All illegal drugs and firearms are strictly prohibited.

Exiting China: Anything made before 1949 is generally considered 'antique' and cannot be taken out of China unless it is certificated. Keep all receipts. NOTE: Taking uncertified antique silver out of China is highly illegal and, if caught smuggling, could result in imprisonment.

Money and Tipping

Foreign Exchange Certificates (FEC), the currency for tourists, was withdrawn from circulation on 1 January 1994. The official currency for everyone is now the 'People's Money', Renminbi (Rmb). This can be exchanged directly for traveller's cheques and currency. The Rmb is issued in denominations of 1, 5, 10, 50 and 100 *yuan*. A *yuan*, popularly known as a *kuai*, is divided into 100 *fen*, with notes of 1, 2, 5, 10, 20 and 50 *fen*. Ten *fen*, called a *jiao* on the banknote, is colloquially referred to as a *mao*.

Renminbi is generally not available outside China, except in Hong Kong where it is now possible to exchange traveller's cheques or foreign currency into Rmb and back. On the black market in China, sophisticated street traders are asking for US dollars with which you can get a better price. However, beware if you are asked to change US dollars to Rmb on the street, you may end up short-changed or with a pocketful of forged notes.

Exchange enough money for your tour of Guizhou in Guiyang—most small towns do not have banks, or if they do, some do not exchange traveller's cheques or foreign currency and the queues can be notoriously long. The Guiyang Park Hotel has a bank which will usually change money or traveller's cheques between 09:00 and 17:00. There is also a Bank of China in the city, five minutes walk from the Plaza, that will change foreign currency and traveller's cheques.

Currently, US$10 is equivalent to 87 *yuan*, HK$100 is equivalent to 112 *yuan* and £10 is equal to 120 *yuan*. Note that these exchange rates do fluctuate.

Tips are expected from all guides and drivers. Tour leaders will make a collection from group members. Individuals could have cigarettes ready to give to those who help them; cigarettes are accepted currency and do help in getting things done. Those visiting villages may bring small gifts but these should be given to the village chiefs.

Post And Telephone

Current postage rates and stamps are available at major hotels in Guiyang. There are post offices in every town. Stamps and envelopes often do not have glue so travellers will find it useful to have a small stick of solid adhesive. International and local telephone calls can be made and faxes sent from the major hotels in Guiyang. The cost of international phone calls are often very high and it is sometimes cheaper to reverse the charges. Local telephone calls can also be made from street telephones; there is usually a telephone sign. Phone links with small towns are poor in Guizhou and it is difficult to get connected.

Health

No compulsory vaccinations are required unless you are coming from an area infected with yellow fever when you must show a vaccination certificate. However, it is wise to be protected against typhoid, hepatitis A, polio, tetanus, rabies and malaria. A detailed brief can be obtained from the the Medical Advisory Service for Travellers Abroad (MASTA) in the UK (tel 0891–224100). Be ready with details of your travel plans to answer questions on a hi-tech recording system and you will be sent a health brief. This takes four to five minutes and costs 36 pence per minute cheap rate, 48 pence at peak times. No similar scheme currently exists in the US, but travellers are advised to consult their own medical practitioner or a travel clinic.

Although cholera is a low risk and the vaccine only gives a 60 per cent protection for three to six months, check for specific outbreaks of cholera. A new strain of cholera (0139 'Bengal') has been reported in Hong Kong and southwest China against which the current vaccine is ineffective. Ensure strict food and water hygiene. All drinking water should be boiled or purified. Malaria has been eliminated from China's major cities and so protection is not necessary on a city tour but, in rural areas of Guizhou, international organizations believe it still exists. Malaria tablets should be taken from July to November to cover yourself. MASTA recommends one tablet weekly (250 miligrams) of a new prescription drug, Mefloquine. Discuss this fully with your travel clinic or doctor before you go. Mefloquine should be strictly avoided during the first three months of pregnancy.

If you are travelling in rural areas, other inoculations you might consider are those against rabies and Japanese encephalitis, a seasonal disease prevalent from June to September. You may wish to carry a sterile needle and syringe pack in the event of an accident to guard against hepatitis B, spread by contaminated needles and blood products. Children could be immunised against TB but it is less important for adults.

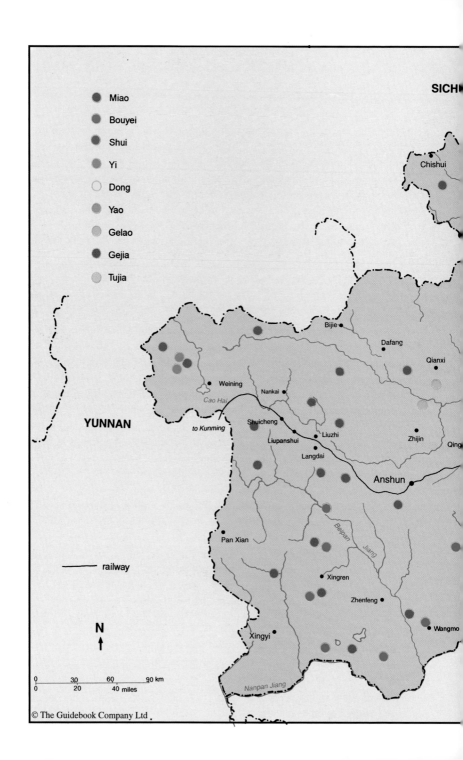

SICH

Chishui

Miao
Bouyei
Shui
Yi
Dong
Yao
Gelao
Gejia
Tujia

Bijie
Dafang
Qianxi

Weining
Cao Hai
Nankai
Shuicheng
to Kunming
Liupanshui
Liuzhi
Zhijin
Qing
Langdai
YUNNAN
Anshun

Pan Xian
Beipan Jiang

railway
Xingren
Zhenfeng

N

Xingyi
Wangmo

0   30   60   90 km
0   20   40 miles
Nanpan Jiang

© The Guidebook Company Ltd

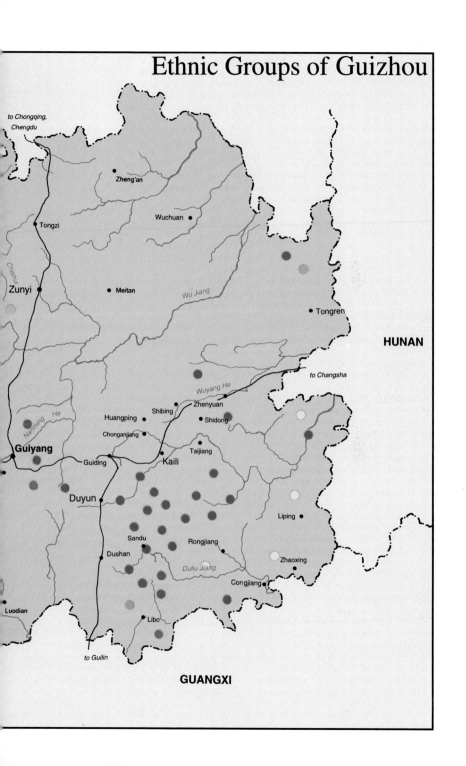

AIDS has been reported in China. The major area of infection is in Yunnan Province, bordering Guizhou, so it is possible that it will spread to Guizhou in the future. Foreign students and nationals staying over one year must produce an HIV antibody test certificate on arrival or undergo a test within 20 days that costs US$30. Testing in the UK or other overseas countries is acceptable but certificates must be notarized and authenticated by the Chinese embassy.

One Province—Diverse People

Guizhou is a cultural melting pot of ethnic groups that have assimilated various characteristics from each other and that continue to pursue their traditional way of life. The mountainous terrain, poor communications and isolation of their communities have, to a large extent, allowed the ethnic groups to preserve their own customs and identity from Han influence. Han Chinese have migrated to Guizhou since the Qin period (221–206 BC) and have become numerically dominant, making up 66 per cent of the total. Han and ethnic people are now often indistinguishable from each other in the urban areas where they wear the same clothes and both speak Chinese.

MAJOR ETHNIC GROUPS WITH A POPULATION OVER 100,000

Miao and Gejia	3,686,900
Bouyei	2,478,100
Dong	1,400,300
Tujia	1,028,200
Yi	707,400
Gelao	430,500
Shui	322,600
Hui	126,500
Bai	122,100

The ethnic languages rely on the spoken word and most have not had a written form until recently. Education, therefore, has been in the Han Chinese script—this has facilitated social mobility since characters are universally understood in China, whatever the dialect or language. Ethnic groups have been brought into the structure of Han Chinese society through education. Since 1979, there have been moves towards a multilingual policy in schools and increasing the status of ethnic languages.

Ethnic identity is a controversial subject. Prior to 1949, ethnic classifications were largely unrecognized and everyone was expected to conform to the Han Chinese model, the largest and most dominant group. After 1949 however, Central Government felt it politically expedient to identify all groups as being socially equal in the new People's Republic. Research teams were sent into the countryside and groups were asked to submit their ethnic identity. Over 400 ethnic groups registered throughout China, of which only 50 were officially recognized. Groups continued to press for independent status. Eventually, 57 ethnic groups were recognized until a review in 1993 added three further groups, all in Guizhou, to the official list. One of these is the Gejia, until now officially considered a subgroup of the Miao. Recognized ethnic groups currently enjoy certain advantages: they can have more than the statutory one child; entrance requirements for university are lower than for Han Chinese; and they are represented at all government administration levels. By acknowledging the ethnic communities (minzu), the Chinese Communist Party felt it could build a stronger, more cohesive state.

This positive discrimination policy has caused a major change. People are now proud of their ethnic status and no longer feel they will be treated unfairly. Between the third and fourth official censuses, the numbers recorded in each ethnic group increased over and above the natural rate of increase, reflecting people's greater willingness to register their ethnic status.

The ethnic groups in Guizhou have a rich culture and important events are celebrated by festivals. There are 365 days in the year but, it is said, over 1,000 festivals (see page 216).

Shopping and Markets

In every city and town daily street markets in designated areas sell high-quality fresh vegetables and fruit brought in by the peasants to sell to the city dwellers. Larger markets, once a week, sell a wider range of goods. The best markets are often on Sundays, a holiday for most workers. One of the most interesting things to do in China is to visit the markets and in Guizhou it is especially interesting as the various ethnic groups mill around in a colourful array of costumes. Each village has its own market on a specific day of the week selling specialities of the area. Visitors can buy locally-made items such as baskets and minority crafts, and a wide range of spices and food products such as water chestnut powder that can be used for thickening.

You can buy a variety of handicrafts—including batiks, musical instruments, embroideries, pottery, lacquerware, herbal medicines, liquor and paintings—from hotel shops or directly from the workshops and factories where they are made. These items, although made throughout the province, are more easily obtained in Guiyang. The major exception to this is ethnic costume and embroidery that is best bought in the villages where they are made or in Kaili.

Guizhou's Culinary Delights: Typical Restaurant Fare

Cold dishes: Tofu, walnuts coated in sugar, pickled beans, pickled mustard.
Main courses: Cold ground rice washed several times with lime to make it set like a jelly and eaten with soy sauce, onions and chilli.
Spicy chicken slices with chilli and onion.
Chilli and pork, well-seasoned especially with ginger.
Sour soup made of fish stock with cabbage and tomato.
Kidney in chilli sauce.
Egg cooked with onion and spices.
Rice.

*****

Cold dishes: Local nuts, pickled cold turnip and mustard.
Main courses: 'Three Star', a mixture of flour, egg, sugar and oil topped with preserved fruit.
Fried liver in chilli sauce.
Chopped pork and peas.
Pickled string beans with chopped pork, chilli and onions.
Boiled pork and vegetables.
Ginkgo fruit served in beaten egg white.
Mustard with hot and sour sauce.
'Three-favourite-soup' made of stock, pork, cabbage, noodles and sea slug.
Rice.

*****

Hot Pot—a winter favourite
Hot Pot can be made with chicken stock cooked on a blazing brazier set into the middle of a low table. Chicken bones and heads bubble away with plenty of ginger, garlic and herbs in the pot. Family or friends sit round and cook their own selection of various thinly-sliced food that is provided in separate dishes. Typical of the dishes are stomach of water buffalo, kidney, liver, tofu, cabbage, bean shoots and transparent bean noodles. After each piece is cooked for a few minutes it is taken out and dipped lavishly in a side plate of chilli and soy sauce. Kidney and liver are highly prized and even more expensive than pork, itself one of the pricier meats.

*****

Dish Dog—a local favourite

Certain restaurants specialize in dog, which is specially bred. It is stir-fried and eaten with vegetables and is particularly welcome in winter for its reputation of keeping you warm. It is also said to help male potency. Dog is one of the most expensive meats and is sometimes chosen as a New Year treat. Visitors are most likely to see dog restaurants at Panjiang, between Guiyang and Kaili. Restaurants line the street and hind quarters are displayed on large plates outside each restaurant.

Cooking in huge woks at a typical small town restaurant

Eating Out in Guizhou

The Chinese greet each other with the words, 'Have you eaten?' and food is always an important topic of conversation at every level of society. The very fact that a centrepiece at a banquet is an exquisite arrangement of foods forming an elaborate picture rather than flowers gives some idea of its significance. Food for special occasions must have a variety of fragrance, indicating freshness and a good blend of seasoning, colour, texture and tastes. In addition, the element of sound, such as crackling, crunching and popping is important. There must be cold starters and hot dishes of chicken, duck, pork and fish with a number of vegetables, a soup, fruits and pastries. A sweet dish may be served mid-meal. At banquets, the rice is served at the end of the meal as a courtesy gesture in case the guest has not had enough to eat. It is not unusual for the host to pick out the best titbits for you, the guest, with his own chopsticks. Chinese banquets are generally conceived to overwhelm guests with food and it is polite to leave some food uneaten. Do not forget to ask your host the names of dishes as even ordinary dishes take on magical names—chicken feet become phoenix claws; pigeons, suckling doves; snake, a dragon or tiger.

Banquets are an experience not to be missed but it is perhaps as much fun to eat at the numerous snack shops and local restaurants that are found in every city and town. Eating out is common in China as it takes some time to get a stove going. People often eat breakfast on their way to work, enjoy bought snacks for lunch and take some ready-cooked dishes home for the family at night, although favourite dishes are usually cooked at home. As a growing number of women join the workforce, more food is bought ready-made and, as in the West, the traditional main meal at midday is being replaced by an evening meal. Restaurants produce the most delicious food, far exceeding some of the best Chinese restaurants in Europe. The only thing lacking is finesse. Local restaurants have no tablecloths or napkins, bones are thrown straight on the floor and there are sounds of general appreciation. Don't be put off as you will be missing a lot. Smarter restaurants are being built as society becomes wealthier and business lunches are becoming an accepted way of life. Guiyang has a number of smart restaurants with good food and charming waitresses dressed in slim-fitting silk *qipaos*.

As part of the 'southwest chilli belt', Guizhou's cuisine shares many characteristics with that of Sichuan, known for its spicy piquancy achieved with the liberal use of chillies, sesame paste, vinegar, Sichuan 'flower pepper', fermented bean paste, scallions (spring onions), ginger, garlic, wine and soy sauce. Guizhou food, however, has its own style. Meals are delicious and full of variety due to the ethnic diversity of the province and the fact that Han Chinese migrated here from all parts of China, bringing with them a wide variety of culinary tastes and skills.

On nearly every street corner stalls offer tasty dishes for the passerby. You can buy a complete meal of rice or wheat noodles topped with crispy pork, pickle and a spoonful of chicken and pork stew. In an everyday meal, it is these staples, rice and wheat, that provide the main calorie intake—an adult easily consumes two to three bowls of rice, topped with small quantities of vegetables, meat or fish. Guizhou's most important snack is bean curd, or tofu, prepared in numerous ways—when toasted on a fire it is known as 'Fall in Love Bean Curd'. Hot chilli sauce is added with a mix of wild garlic shoots, soy sauce and vinegar. Bean curd can also be served with cooked beans and sour pickled cabbage. A winter favourite is sizzling beef kebabs, peppered well, cooked over charcoal fires and sprinkled with sesame seed. This particular dish was introduced by the Uyghurs from Xinjiang who migrated to Guiyang. Lamb is used in their home province but as the local Chinese dislike lamb and beef is cheaper, the dish has been adapted. Other vendors stir-fry great woks of steamed glutinous rice with egg sheets. Soy sauce, vinegar and the all-important onions are added for a tasty snack.

Those wanting a sweet snack can eat steamed glutinous rice, pounded to a sticky dough and then rolled in sugar and spices or filled with sweetmeat and deep-fried. Vendors neatly take your money and give you change with a pair of chopsticks. 'Eight Treasures', a wonderful snack for those with a sweet tooth, consists of sweet soup thickened with water chestnut flour. To this is added sesame seed, glacé fruits, dates, prunes, quail eggs, red glutinous rice, raisins, preserved apricots, preserved white gourd and lotus seeds. This is a complete meal in itself. Young children love deep fried potatoes served with chilli sauce. Water chestnuts are equally delicious roasted hot or cold. Western-style sponge cakes with sticky icing are on offer alongside local snacks like sugar-coated walnuts, a sweetened green paste made from beans and a nougat-like delicacy made from rice flour, sugar and nuts.

Young couples frequent the night markets that are found in most towns and cities. Since 1980, private traders have been allowed to re-establish stalls in designated areas and sell what the Chinese like best—food. Competition is fierce. On a typical evening out you can begin with yoghurt, then move on to a stall selling roast chicken. Choose your favourite piece, be it a leg or wing but, remember, heads and feet are popular too—chicken claws are said to bring money and fortune. Each piece is dipped in a rich brown sauce of soya, chilli, onion and wild pepper and fried. Rice pot is particularly popular, prepared by pouring oil into clay pots that are placed on the fire. The rice is then added with beans, peas or potatoes and the mixture topped with barbecued pork pieces and served piping hot. The rice at the bottom is deliciously crispy. A cold salad of various well-spiced roots is served with it. You can then try bean sprouts, pickled mustard and string beans followed by a delicately-flavoured cabbage soup to cool the mouth. Next you could sample pink pomelo,

Chillies for sale at Weining market

carefully peeled and prepared. Scalloped pineapples from south Yunnan, served on sticks, are also fresh and tasty. Numerous steamed dumplings are filled with savoury meats and vegetables and cooked in a boiling pot of broth. Other stalls display pork delicacies or whole highly-flavoured waxy salty ducks that have been plucked, pulled, salted, flattened by smashing the breast bone with a meat cleaver and then hung in the sun to dry. Twisty spiky stomachs vie with split tongues and hearts lie beside round fatty sausages. The local entertainment of 'eating your way home' is a lot of fun and certainly worth experiencing.

Central Guizhou

Central Guizhou is centred on Guiyang, the provincial capital, and Anshun. The two cities are the industrial heartland and the most sophisticated areas of the province.

Guiyang

Guiyang, easily the largest city in the province, means 'precious sunshine' and is nicknamed 'second spring city'. The city lies in a basin at 1,071 metres (3,514 feet) on the Nanming River and is surrounded by mountains. The population of nearly 1 million is divided into 87 per cent Han Chinese and 13 per cent ethnic groups.

The old walled city of Guiyang was built during the Ming Dynasty (1368–1644) according to the rules of geomancy, south of the mountain and north of the river. Then and during the Qing Dynasty (1644–1911), Guiyang was a small administrative town situated around Huaxi. It became capital of Guizhou in 1913. In March 1935, Chiang Kai-shek flew to the province to direct operations against Mao Ze Dong who, he believed, was about to take the city. Instead, Mao slipped away towards the east with the Red Army and the city remained undisturbed until it was bombed by Japanese planes in 1939, destroying a third of the old city. Guiyang was established as a municipality in 1941 but, because of its remoteness, remained a small backward town. Between 1944 and 1945, during the war with Japan, it became the centre of Nationalist Government activities. People flocked to Guiyang from all parts of the country and a university was founded. After 1945, Chongqing took over as headquarters for the Kuomintang, but by this time, Guiyang was on the map and its development had begun. The highest building in 1949 was five storeys and the main transport was the horse and carriage. Today, the Park Hotel has 31 storeys, there is a good transport network and Guiyang is the main industrial city of Guizhou, producing 35 per cent of the total industrial output of the province.

Locally-mined coal and hydroelectricity form the basis of Guiyang's power industry. One factory utilises local tobacco to produce a wide range of cigarettes including medicinal ones. An aluminium plant mines, smelts and processes local bauxite. Chemicals, fertilizers and plastics are also produced. Local cotton and synthetic yarn is woven and there is a growing garment trade. Paper is made from timber cut in the province. Various machinery is being produced with iron and steel; large corporations are manufacturing diggers, trucks, tractors and small buses. Automobile production will become very important in the future. Food and wine processing, including Maotai, cement and building materials, and recent hi-tech industries such as electronic precision instruments and optics are all contributing to the industrial development of this expanding city. Guiyang is also home to a wide range of educational institutes including universities, academies, research centres, medical and teacher-training colleges. It boasts sufficient entertainment to delight any visitor. Choose from ten theatres, the provincial and municipal song and dance troupes, numerous local opera including the Peking and Guizhou operas, a circus troupe, cinemas and discos. Here, modern and age-old forms of entertainment blend—one local resident notes 'there are three main entertainments in Guiyang for the young—gossiping, disco dancing and mahjong'.

GETTING THERE

Guiyang is the nodal centre for roads and railways that connect Guizhou with all parts of China, in particular Sichuan, Yunnan, Guangxi and Guangdong provinces. Travellers can get to Guiyang easily from most parts of China. Guiyang Airport is situated at Huaxi with connecting flights to other cities in China. You can now fly direct to Guiyang from Hong Kong (see page 26). A new airport, due to open in 1996, is being built eight kilometres (five miles) outside the city at Longdongbao.

SITES IN GUIYANG

The numerous local buses serve as a convenient and easy way to get around Guiyang. Ask advice and for bus numbers from reception before leaving your hotel. Local taxis can be flagged down in the street and most do have meters. Taxis are available at the major hotels or you can sometimes hire a car and driver through reception. Non-Chinese speakers might find it a good idea to carry the name of your hotel in Chinese characters so you can easily get back.

■ QIANLING PARK AND HONGFU TEMPLE (OPENING HOURS: 06:00–22:00)
This cool, quiet park covers 300 hectares (741 acres) in the northwest of the city. It is worth a visit for its beautiful lake, offering boating and swimming, and for the fine ancient trees, bustling with wild and tame monkeys. Walk from the park gates up Nine-Twisting Path to the top of Mount Qianling, crowned by the Zen Buddhist temple, Hongfu (Temple of Good Fortune), originally built in 1673 by the monk Chishong. The ravages of the Cultural Revolution destroyed most of the original buildings and some of the graves of the abbots; it has since been tastefully restored. Buddhist artists work on fine calligraphy in the temple complex. This is a refuge from the heat of the city where monkeys play and birds soar in the sky, and it offers good views of Guiyang. A beautifully presented vegetarian banquet of outstanding quality can be arranged at Hongfu Temple. There is also a small zoo in the grounds of the park housing pandas and other animals.

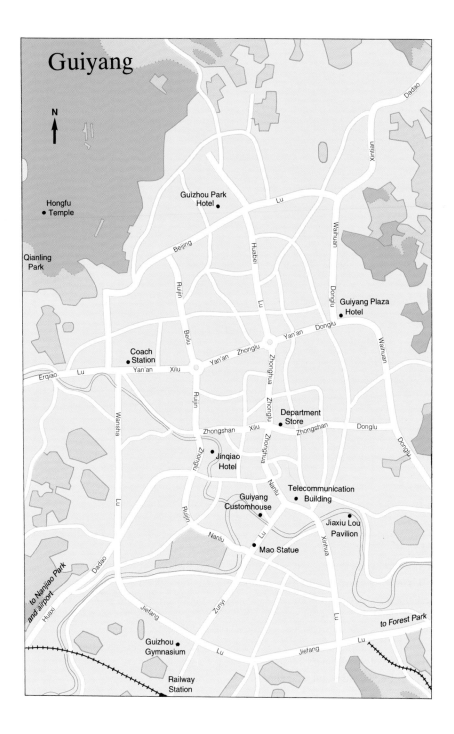

■ FOREST PARK (OPENING HOURS: 08:00–18:00)
Eight kilometres (five miles) southeast of the city centre, this 270-hectare (667-acre) park offers wonderful walks along a ridge densely covered with huge old tea bushes, resembling tall trees. Sadly, it is now too expensive to produce the tea oil that was much prized for cooking because of its unique flavour.

The Chinese picnic here on their days off, especially on Sundays, and drink tea while listening to the cicadas.

■ BOTANICAL GARDENS OF GUIZHOU
Founded in 1964 and open to the public, the gardens cover 88 hectares (217 acres) at a height of 1,210–1,410 metres (3,970–4,626 feet). For those interested in plants and trees, this is well worth a visit.

Scientists in charge of the gardens focus on research into wild plant resources and the introduction and cultivation of new, medicinal, ornamental, rare and endangered species. Specialists will gain the greatest advantage by prearranging their visit. In contrast to many Western botanical gardens, these are not landscaped.

■ NANJIAO PARK AND WHITE DRAGON CAVE
This cave, lit with neon lights, is in the centre of a small park to the south of Guiyang city. You walk on stepping stones through the cave, which extends for 587 metres (1,926 feet), across a large lake. If you are visiting larger limestone caves elsewhere in the province this particular cave is not really worth your time.

■ JIAXIU LOU (FIRST SCHOLAR'S) PAVILION (OPENING HOURS: 09:00–18:00)
Built in 1587, this beautiful Ming-dynasty three-storey tower rises 20 metres (66 feet) up on Fu-yu Bridge over the Nanming River. Its original purpose was to encourage young scholars to meet together each year at the provincial Confucian examinations. The present exhibition of old furniture and stone tablets inscribed with poems makes it a charming place to visit.

■ PROVINCIAL MUSEUM
Temporary exhibitions are held on the ground floor while the first floor houses a general exhibition of Guizhou's natural resources and an interesting display of archaeological finds of the area. In particular, there are several outstanding grave finds of the Han period (206 BC–220 AD). Don't miss the well-planned section on ethnic costume and related material that presents the lifestyle of the people.

■ STATUE OF CHAIRMAN MAO ZE DONG
One of the few remaining Socialist statues of Mao stands in the People's Square.

■ RELIGIOUS BUILDINGS

The Catholic Church (Heping Road, off Putuo Road) The church, reopened after the Cultural Revolution (1966–1976), holds services on Sundays that are attended by over 1,000 people. The exterior resembles a traditional Chinese temple.

Guiyang Christian Church (West Qianling Road) This is the only church remaining of the four originally established in Guiyang by the China Inland Mission. It was rebuilt in 1982 and its interior is a large hall devoid of any ornamentation. Over 1,000 people attend on Sundays.

Yang Ming Temple (Yang Ming Road) This well-restored Buddhist temple, rebuilt in 1771, is worth a visit. Its active community meets regularly to study Buddhist texts. Businessmen have reinstated the practice of contributing to the temple to gain merit. You approach the temple through a charming bird and goldfish market.

■ SI YUE BA MINORITY FESTIVAL

On the eighth day of the fourth lunar month, Miao ethnic people from the surrounding area flock to the city centre and parade around the fountain in their festival costumes. The festival, accompanied by singing and dancing to lusheng pipes, is held in memory of two Miao heroes, Gelubo and Zudelong, who died fighting in the uprisings against the Han Chinese.

SHOPPING

Guizhou is a veritable treasure house of handicrafts. Look for the wide variety of products at the hotel shops in Guiyang, the Cultural Relics Store, the Nationalities Department Store and the Overseas Chinese Friendship Store.

■ BATIK

The Miao and Bouyei are very skilled in the craft of batik. Local artists, inspired by traditional ethnic designs, have produced an interesting range of modern batik wall hangings.

■ YUPING FLUTES

These flutes, made in northeast Guizhou, are known throughout China for their quality and have won international awards.

■ TRADITIONAL MIAO AND BOUYEI EMBROIDERY AND JEWELLERY

Outstanding examples of embroidery and full costumes are available in Guiyang, but they are usually cheaper in the countryside and villages. Copies of traditional silver jewellery in base metal make interesting gifts and souvenirs. Please note that real silver must not be taken out of China unless authorized with an official seal.

Full Moon Festivities

In the spring of 1894, after making enquiries for two years, we were able to be present at one of the Aboriginal festivals. Our coal and coke merchant, a Chinaman, invited us to his village home for the occasion, where his wife generously entertained our party. The festival took place at the full moon in March on a small plateau encircled by hill tops. We started after breakfast the day before full moon, and a few miles beyond Kuei-yang began ascending the hills, by midday reaching a wayside inn, where we had eggs poached in sugar and water. Here my husband left us to return to the city, while our road led us over barren hills whose valleys had opium, vegetable, oil, and bean plants, with waste places for sowing rice. The road was so bad that often we had to get out of the sedans and walk, and only reached the plateau by dark. We were given a good-sized room, but soon found that the Aboriginal guests, mothers and daughters, had the right of way through it.

Next morning we watched the girls adorning themselves, they spent four hours at their toilette. The dress consisted of several suits of a very dark colour, the outer garments being a loose jacket, open in front like a sailor's, and a closely (accordion) pleated skirt, resembling a kilt, and like it reaching to just below the knee. The jackets were beautifully embroidered with coloured silks, and the skirt, seven yards wide, was also embroidered. Their hair was coiled slightly to one side and partly hidden by the number of broad-headed silver pins used, and all wore three or four silver necklaces.

At noon the dance began, from between the conical hills lads and lasses of sixteen to twenty years old came running down to the plateau, the youths wearing dark-coloured robes of various shades, girded with embroidered sashes crossed in front and folded at the back, and like the girls they had silver ornaments in their hair, while both had tassels or streamers falling down their backs; the youths also carried a six-tubed flute whose music resembles the bass of a harmonium.

In the centre of the plateau was a high pole, and round this sat the mothers; while forming a great circle around them were the youths and maidens, standing in groups of usually four maidens and three youths, outside these was another circle, and then a third one, making in all 400 dancers. At a given signal the lads played a few bars, and then waving their flutes in unison, each little group moved sideways on a few steps, the lassies taking the lead until they stopped, when the lads would play another few bars and then the group moved again. In this way all the groups moved on so that in time the whole circle and the other two circles had gone round the pole; and this the circles did several times until nearly sunset, when as they dispersed there was a general exchanging of necklaces, and we noticed that one lucky youth had twenty round his neck, so that he could hardly turn his head, but I could not speak their language to ask how he had got such a number.

The maidens staying at the house where we were came back for their evening meal, which only consisted of coarse red rice and dried beans fried in vegetable oil; but after supper the youths from other houses came serenading their sweethearts and soon we heard a general stampede. This dance and evening serenade continued for two more days, and then they all journeyed homewards till next year. The dance is held in the same place for three years running, when a new site is chosen.

Mrs Pruen, The Provinces of Western China, 1906

■ JINZHU GLAZED POTTERY
Developed from the local Yazhou pottery, this is used mainly for daily necessities such as kettles, bowls, plates, lamps, incense burners and toys. Yellow and green are the dominant colours.

■ XIONGJING SCULPTURES
Human and animal figures as well as flowers and birds form part of the traditional art of Guizhou.

■ ZHIJIN INK HOLDERS
Chinese brush painters will find these ink holders, made of local marble, a worthwhile purchase.

■ GUIZHOU LACQUERWARE
Made in Dafang, this lacquerware is particularly attractive.

■ WOODEN OPERA MASKS
Masks for Ground Opera, previously produced in Bouyei and Laohan villages by local craftsmen for their own use, are now being made commercially in a few villages around Anshun for sale in Guiyang and elsewhere in China. Nuo Opera, practised only in very remote areas of northeast Guizhou, uses different masks with crooked faces and distorted eyes and mouths. These are being copied for commercial sale.

■ CIGARETTES
Guizhou is one of four tobacco-producing centres in China. Huangguoshu, Zunyi, Guiyang, Huaxi and Yunwushan are all famous brand names produced by the Guiyang Cigarette Factory.

■ LIQUORS
Guizhou is known for its quality liquors that enjoy both national and international fame, such as Maotai, Dongjiu, Xishui Daqu, Pingba Jiaojiu and Yaxi Jiaojiu.

■ TEA
Guizhou Province has a rich resource of first-class tea.

STREET MARKETS
One of the most enjoyable experiences in Guiyang is exploring the backstreets and markets such as the **bird and ornamental fish market**. Visit the **food market** along Fushui Street (Xiaoshizi area) after 17:00 when the local people enjoy eating their

evening meal at a variety of stalls. Sample the tremendous variety of snacks, especially duck, and soak up the local atmosphere. Other side streets throughout the city provide interesting snacks. Miao sour soup is served along Putuo Road and dog in Shachong Street.

AROUND GUIYANG

■ HUAXI PARK (OPENING HOURS 07:00–18:00)

Enjoy beautiful walks along the river and on Linshan Mountain at this park, 17 kilometres (10.5 miles) from Guiyang on the southern outskirts. The Chinese come here to picnic and swim. The old mill has been converted to an artists' studio that sells a variety of modern paintings and sculpture, depending on who is working in the studio at the time. Artists and sculptors live and work in nearby villages—ask for information when you are there as exhibits are always changing.

■ BAIHUA LAKE

This attractive lake, set in limestone hills, is 22 kilometres (13.6 miles) from Guiyang. You can hire a boatman to row you across the lake. It is very peaceful here.

■ HONGFENG (RED MAPLE) LAKE

Pretty islands and clear blue lakes cover an area of 57 square kilometres (22 square miles), 37 kilometres (23 miles) from Guiyang. It is ideal for boating around the small islands. A Dong village has recently been reconstructed in concrete at the lakeside to attract foreign tourists. If possible, visit the authentic Dong areas rather than make do with this copy.

■ HUANGGUOSHU WATERFALL

You can visit the waterfall from Guiyang on a day trip, 150 kilometres (93 miles) along the new toll road, or more easily from Anshun (see page 62).

■ ZHIJIN CAVE

China's largest limestone cave complex, known as the 'King of Caves', is 180 kilometres (112 miles) northwest of Guiyang and 120 kilometres (75 miles) from Anshun. In some places it reaches a height of 154 metres (505 feet) and a width of 170 metres (558 feet). You can walk at least 10 kilometres (6 miles) through a magnificent display of stalactites and stalagmites. A Chinese poet wrote in 1988: 'You don't want to see other mountains when you return from Huangshan and there is no other cave in your heart after you have seen Zhijin Cave'. At the moment, it is a long day's journey from Guiyang on a narrow and winding road. Very basic accommodation is available at the county town of Zhijin.

(following pages) *The 'King of Caves' at Zhijin*

■ ETHNIC VILLAGES

You can visit Miao and Bouyei villages from Guiyang, sample the tremendous hospitality of the ethnic people and take part in their drinking ceremonies. Villagers dress up in magnificent festival clothes and will dance and sing traditional songs as well as offer a meal. One Bouyei village is planning to show tourists a traditional marriage ceremony—ask at GZOTC or CITS as all arrangements must be made through these offices. More adventurous travellers can visit villages not frequented by tourists.

SUGGESTED TOUR ITINERARY

Guiyang is the starting point for a southwest China tour. A rewarding itinerary can be organized from Guiyang taking in both the spectacular karst landscape features and the ethnic villages. Stay at least two nights in Guiyang and visit some of the city sights. You can arrange to see a Miao village and then travel out to Huangguoshu Waterfall—spend a day walking in the waterfall area amid spectacular landforms. Visit a Bouyei and Miao village in the area and return to Guiyang before leaving for other parts of China. Guizhou enthusiasts will make this a jumping-off point for seeing other parts of the province.

Anshun

Anshun is linked to Guiyang by a new major highway, a journey that takes only two hours. This is a great improvement on two years ago when the road was narrow and twisting and it took four to six hours.

Anshun is an old established trading centre going back to the 13th century and linking north and south China with areas as remote as Burma via Kunming. It is described by the Chinese as 'the throat to Yunnan and the belly of Guizhou'. Tea was exported through Anshun but merchants gained a bad reputation for substituting willow leaves. Later, opium was added to its list of exports—Guizhou was one of the largest growers of the opium poppy in the 19th and early 20th centuries. Anshun continued as an important commercial and minor industrial centre until 1949.

The industrial base today has greatly expanded due to rich coal reserves that have provided an excellent energy source. Heavy machinery, aeroplanes, food processing, distilling and the leather industry are particularly important. Aeroplane manufacture was the direct result of Mao Ze Dong's decentralization of industry. An important industrial defence complex is located in the Anshun area.

Anshun is praised for its excellent cuisine. Ask advice from local people who will guide you to the current best restaurants.

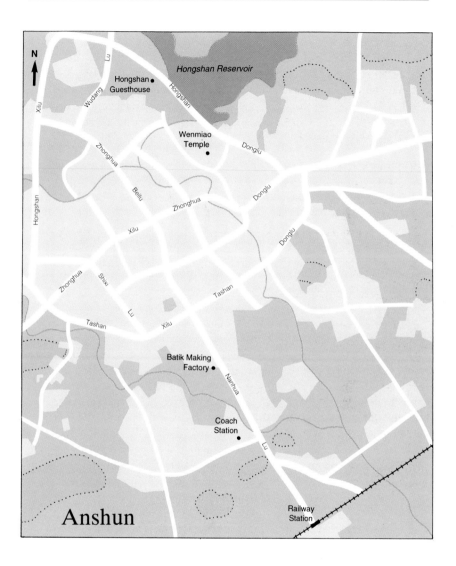

Anshun

SITES IN AND AROUND ANSHUN

■ THE WHITE PAGODA

The first of this city's pagodas dates from the Ming Dynasty (1368–1644) and is a symbol of Anshun. It is decorated with carved Buddhist scriptures to expel the evil spirits and ghosts that haunted the surrounding mountains.

■ WEN MIAO TEMPLE
Built in 1368, this temple was originally covered with finely-carved figures depicting the Confucian education system, some of which remain.

■ TIAN TAI SHAN BUDDHIST TEMPLE
To the northeast of Anshun off the new toll road to Guiyang, near Pingba, this temple was rebuilt on a limestone buttress in the 1920s but dates back to 1616. There is no regular bus service to the temple but a minibus park is situated midway up the hill; from there it is a five minute walk to the gates of the temple. During the Cultural Revolution the temple was ransacked. Today the inner temples are being restored with new gilded Buddhas and a Ground Opera (Dixi) Museum has been established, although this is rather dusty and badly displayed.

■ HUANGGUOSHU WATERFALL AND LONGGONG (DRAGON PALACE) CAVE
Visit Longgong Cave first on the way to Huangguoshu, southwest of Anshun. The cave stretches for 15 kilometres (9 miles) and a boat ride gives an enjoyable view of part of the cave that is illuminated. There are excellent walks in the area on well-made paths.

After lunch, travel through superb karst limestone scenery and green or golden paddy fields, depending on the season, to Huangguoshu Waterfall. The waterfall is fed by the Baishui and Dabang rivers; along their length are another 19 waterfalls and nine cascades. The spectacular major fall, the biggest in Asia, is over 68 metres (223 feet) high and 84 metres (276 feet) wide. Its continuous flow of water varies in volume with the season and the control of water in the reservoir behind the fall. On a sunny day the sight is especially beautiful as a rainbow arches over the falls. A well-cut cliff path has been built behind the fall from where you get a beautiful view of the water curtain. There are walks in the area below the falls near Tianxingqiao Bridge among rocks of strange shape and deep, still pools. Remember to take mosquito repellent.

■ ETHNIC VILLAGES
Visit Bouyei, Laohan and Miao villages in the area. Their traditional clothes incorporate outstanding embroidery and batik. Demonstrations of these skills can be arranged as well as superb traditional song and dance performances when the people dress in their festival costume. If you prefer not to make special arrangements, it is still of great interest to watch the people working in the fields at the daily tasks that have hardly changed for centuries. Water buffalo pull wooden ploughshares, men and women plant rice then sickle and thresh by hand. Many of the women still dress in traditional costume.

TEA: THE ESSENCE OF LIFE

Tea drinking is an essential part of everyday Chinese life and a very wide range of tea is grown, each with its own special flavour and properties. You will see the tender shoots being carefully picked from rows of tea bushes by women in many areas of Guizhou—large tea plantations are established between Huangguoshu and Guiyang, in the environs of Duyun and in other areas of the south. The tea merchants of Anshun had a particularly bad reputation in the past for adding willow leaves to the tea they sold. Tea is generally sold unfermented and green; fragrance is sometimes gained by adding various flowers such as jasmine or, in the spring, honeysuckle flowers. In the larger cities you will find shops specializing in the sale of local tea and that from other areas of China. Choosing the right tea for a special occasion can be a lengthy affair, as a connoiseur in Europe might choose a wine. Prices generally vary from 10 to 24 *yuan* for 500 grams (1.1 pounds), but particularly well-known teas sell for 200 *yuan*, such as the local Mao Jian tea from Duyun while Mei Jiang tea grown near Zunyi is even more expensive at 250 *yuan* for 500 grams (1.1 pounds). Tea is beautifully packaged and enjoys a thriving market in Japan and with overseas Chinese.

An old saying suggests 'one can live without grain for a day, but cannot do without tea'. Tea-drinking habits and traditions vary from place to place but careful preparation is always considered vital. Mountain spring water is regarded as best for brewing tea as it contains minerals that give a subtle flavour. Su Shi, a famous scholar of the Song Dynasty (960–1279) and an expert in the art of tea, often said, 'live water should be boiled by a live fire'. Water should be boiled, quickly taken off the fire and then added to the leaves. Tea should be sipped slowly while it is still hot so the fragrance can be tasted. It is, in fact, considered vulgar to drink too quickly.

A meal in a restaurant always starts with tea, and drivers and travellers usually carry a jar of tea with a screw lid that is filled with hot water at every stop to make the leaves last all day. Peasants offer you tea as you pass by their homes and, if they are too poor to buy tea, they will serve hot water, known as 'white tea'. Some of the most interesting teas are those of the Dong minority—you can sample these at the Tea Ceremony at the Dragon River Hotel in Duyun. Many claims are made for teas, including promoting the production of body fluid, removing phlegm, improving eyesight, replenishing vital energy, reducing fat, calming nervous complaints and preventing cancer.

Tea plantation outside Anshun

SHOPPING

You can visit the Anshun General Batik Factory to watch batik being produced by hand and to buy cloth. This is a relatively new factory, producing cotton textiles in a wide variety of imaginative designs. These designs are inspired by those of the local ethnic people, adapted and utilised by modern artists. A number of Japanese designs are also manufactured.

Modern batik cloth is sold in lengths or made up into women's clothes and bags. Designs are generally large and bold and the colours bright. There are some attractive blue and white designs. All are chemically dyed and have the disadvantage of not being colourfast. It is interesting to compare commercial and village production.

Shops within the complex, often run by people from Guilin, sell a variety of antiques, herbal medicines, paintings and ethnic costume as well as batik cloth. However, take note that prices are generally high.

A Tall-Pointed Hat Miao Lusheng Festival

A steady stream of young and old men, women and children hurry along the main road 30 kilometres (19 miles) from Anshun in late February. The road runs between terraced fields, clothed in luminescent yellow rape flowers and delicate mauve turnip flowers. Rounded limestone hills, silhouetted against an inky-grey sky, fringe the scene. The people are going to the local Miao festival of **Tiao Hua Chang**, held on the 12th, 13th and 14th days of the first lunar month. The older men in blue cotton Mao suits are outnumbered by young men in tight-fitting trousers and flapping brown and black Western-style jackets. Young children in brightly coloured coats and trousers walk alongside mothers still dressed traditionally in dark jackets and swinging blue pleated skirts edged with white, their legs wrapped in blue braid. Their height is exaggerated by tall pointed blue hats covering shaved heads and indicating marital status. Bundles strapped to the women's backs cascade upwards into what seems like exotic blue flowers tinged at the edges with white. These are the precious new pleated skirts for their daughters to wear at the festival. They clutch plastic bags containing silver ornaments and embroidered pieces. As they swing along with the crowd they chat to their daughters, dressed for the moment in light blouses and sweaters. The girls' hair is often long and held back in a pony tail or frizzed with a permanent wave.

The appointed festival ground, known as the Flower Ground, is set in the middle of the rocky hillside surrounded by rape fields. Thousands of people mill around waiting for the ceremony to begin. Young Han Chinese and some Miao villagers in modern city clothes, the girls in high heels, wander up the central track that is lined with vendors selling their wares. There are plastic toys for the children; glass rattles; a selection of ribbons and hair slides for the girls; fruit, particularly small tangerines and bright oranges, bananas and pears; piles of peanuts and sunflower seeds; and sugar cane, sweets and biscuits. Stalls have been set up as far as you can see where men and women are busily preparing snacks for the crowd to eat—popular dishes include hot noodles with crispy pork spiced with peppers and soy sauce, and rice and bean jelly sliced into thin strips and served with vinegar, soy sauce and ground red chilli.

The day is hot so most of the crowd just sit, smoke and chat but a lively traditional opera performed by a Bouyei group from a nearby village creates

tremendous interest. Villagers press in a tight circle around the male performers who are dressed in the colourful robes of Ming period (1368–
1644) soldiers, their foreheads covered by brightly painted masks. Long
feathers attached to the masks nod furiously as the actors gesticulate and
simulate the ancient military plot. There are acrobatics too and mock
battles with wooden tasselled spears. The crowd laughs at well-known
jokes and the performance continues to the sound of the drum.

In a quiet corner the Miao womenfolk are gathering with their daughters' costumes; many also hold carefully-wrapped, beautifully embroidered
baby carriers. Now is the time to start dressing their daughters and sons in
their finery for the parade. The unmarried girls don long pleated skirts and
jackets, wrapping tight cummerbunds around their waists and arranging
their two-pointed hats. Silver jewellery, in particular beautiful necklaces
and bracelets, are adjusted. Unmarried boys from the age of 11 to 20 are
being robed in blue satin or cotton gowns. Their waists are also bound with
a tight cummerbund but, of greater significance, is the headdress made of
hand-woven chequered blue cloth wound tightly round and round the
head. A silver locket on a chain is looped over a second plain silver necklace. Brightly embroidered strips corded together are tied round the waist.

Finally, the boys and girls gather together in village groups, the older
boys in front playing the lusheng pipes. These groups parade rather shyly
in one large circle around the Flower Ground while the onlookers crowd in
to admire the beautifully-dressed young people. They parade only for a
short time and then disband, after which everybody goes to visit friends.
The Miao villages are lively until the early hours of morning with drinking,
eating, gossiping and socializing. Families stay with relatives or friends,
giving the young the opportunity to meet girls and boys from different
villages and thus to find a marriage partner. For everyone, the festival is
about having fun and catching up with news from those who have come
from afar to attend.

In the village, an old man explains the origins of the Tiao Hua Chang
festival, typical of the Miao's rich wealth of oral folk tales. 'Far back in the
past an old man, Liu Yao Lu, had two attractive daughters. One day they
were walking in the mountains when suddenly a tiger appeared and seized
one of the girls in his mouth. The other girl ran away as quickly as possible.
The incident was witnessed by Zhou Zhi Gou who was considered a particularly brave man in the area with special powers. Zhou followed the tiger

and, because of his superhuman strength, rescued the girl and told her to go home.

On his way back to the village, Zhou lost a shoe in a stream. This shoe was found by the rescued girl's father, who on hearing the story, retraced her footsteps in an attempt to find and thank the unknown rescuer and to offer him his daughter in marriage as a reward. Because Liu was the headman of the village, he had the authority to organize a festival. Lusheng players came, the dancing began and each young man of the village tried on the shoe but, alas, it did not fit any of them.

Zhou, meanwhile, was sleeping at home, exhausted after his encounter, until a relative called to tell him about the festival. On the 49th day he went to the celebrations and tried on the shoe. It fitted and Liu gave his daughter's hand in marriage to Zhou. The entire village paid their respects to Zhou for his bravery and he and his father-in-law kept the peace in the area so that the village prospered.

This lusheng festival is celebrated every year in memory of Zhou.'

An unmarried Tall-Pointed Hat Miao girl dressed for a festival

Southeast Guizhou

This is the area of Guizhou most frequented by tourists. However, the majority concentrate on Kaili city and the few ethnic villages in the immediate vicinity, thereby missing out on many fascinating areas only a short drive away from the city. If you are prepared to stay at smaller centres and in Chinese-style hotels, there is much to see. The landscape is very attractive, with its terraced rice paddies and extensive karst scenery, but perhaps the main reason for travelling to this area is to explore the fascinating Miao and Dong areas.

Kaili

Kaili city is the capital of the Miao and Dong Autonomous Prefecture of southeast Guizhou. Ethnic people account for 70 per cent of the population of this area. In and around Kaili itself there are a number of industries that include building materials, textiles, paper-making, electronics and engineering.

SITES IN AND AROUND KAILI

■ KAILI MUSEUM (OPENING HOURS: 10:00–17:00, MONDAY–SATURDAY)
A very extensive museum giving an interesting overview of the ethnic people of the area with original photos and costumes. Also featured is the development of agriculture and industry in the prefecture.

■ GU LOU DRUM TOWER
Rebuilt in 1985 in traditional Dong style, this cleverly-constructed tower is made entirely without metal nails. Villagers meet here on special occasions for songs and dances.

■ XIANG LU (INCENSE POT) MOUNTAIN
Shaped like an incense burner, this mountain stands outside the town and has become a symbol of Kaili. It was nearby that the Miao hero Zhang Xiu Mei was defeated by the Han Chinese in the mid-19th century. An annual festival held during the sixth lunar month commemorates his death during which local people climb the mountain.

■ ETHNIC VILLAGES
There are a number of Miao and Gejia villages a short distance from Kaili open to visitors. Arrangements to visit can be made through the Guiyang tourist organizations or through CITS in Kaili.

THE SUNDAY MARKET

This lively market is definitely worth a visit. Because many Miao people live nearby, Kaili's market provides the added interest of traditionally dressed Miao girls and women. There is a growing tendency for Miao girls to dress like the Han Chinese girls in trousers and jackets, rather than in their black pleated skirts and embroidered jackets. However, they nearly always wear their hair in a traditional manner piled high according to the style of their village and decorated with plastic combs, ribbons and even plastic flowers instead of silver.

The vegetable and fresh food section varies according to the season but there is a profusion of fresh vegetables year-round that far outstrips any local European market. In spring there are bamboo baskets full of a wide assortment of mushrooms and fungi. There are basketloads of fresh cabbage of different varieties, plenty of red tomatoes, neat bundles of mustard plant, big white flowery cauliflowers, fresh garlic shoots, Chinese lettuces used for hotpot, pea shoots, wild garlic, mountains of dried red chillies and cloves of garlic. Most intriguing are large wooden barrels full of delicate yellow-green bean shoots, freshly sprouted. These contrast with piles of dried twisted seaweed. Autumn brings more tomatoes, bamboo shoots, aubergines (eggplant), gourds and cucumber-like plants. There are earth melons that look like white turnips, peeled and eaten raw as a quick snack. Sweet and Irish potatoes are sold.

Don't miss the herb section. Root ginger is always on sale along with bags of all the spices that make up Chinese five-spice; dried chilli, plenty of wild pepper and a range of other seeds and spices. Wood ginger, a delicate yellow flower on a bare branch, is available in spring and is delicious with pork or chicken. There are always bundles of fresh green herbs, especially coriander.

The meat section is nearby. Freshly-killed pork, the most popular meat, is often brought to market as a complete carcass slung over a bicycle. Numerous stalls sell every conceivable item of the animal's anatomy—nothing is wasted in China. There is a spectacular array of stomach, intestines, liver, kidneys, head, lungs and ears. Beef is now popular and is cheaper than pork. Beautiful bamboo baskets contain live chickens. The locals prefer to buy fresh for the pot. You might see the throats of live chickens being cut; the blood is collected in a large bowl and the bird is put into boiling fat and then covered in black tar so it can be plucked quickly, ready for sale. Small piglets are paraded on strings or carefully encased in hand-woven bamboo containers designed for their size and shape.

Chicken, duck or spotted quails' eggs are displayed alongside popular 'thousand-year eggs', still coated with the lime in which they have been buried for 40 days that turns the yolks bright orange and the whites a gelatinous opaque substance. Surprisingly, the fish at Kaili is not fresh but frozen.

Not far away are all sorts of noodles—fresh and dried wheat noodles, translucent bean and rice noodles along with canna lily noodles made from the starchy rhizome. Every form of tofu can be found since it is one of the most important forms of protein.

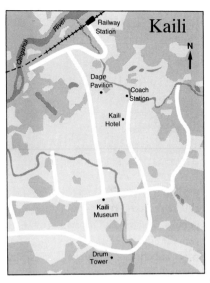

A wide range of fruit is always at the market: apples and pears in the autumn; bananas, oranges and tangerines, grown in south Guizhou, in the winter and spring. Autumn also brings orange persimmons, giant pomelos and Chinese gooseberry or monkey peach. Plenty grow wild in the province and are especially valuable as a source of vitamin C. There are always piles of peanuts and sunflower seeds to nibble. Cracking sunflower seeds between your teeth is a very popular way to pass the time; some Chinese have worn their front teeth down into a notch.

To satisfy the needs of the many local people who have travelled quite a distance to the market, there are plenty of snack stalls. Steamed buns are kept hot over a steamer. One of the favourites is toasted bean curd, served with various sauces and always plenty of chilli, often served rather like a sandwich. Nearly everyone nibbles on sugar cane. Spicy kebabs and brown gelatinous taro is served heated on a skewer and eaten with cold pickles and spices. Those wanting a larger meal can choose a bowl of noodles with various spicy meat toppings. Rice cakes filled with herbs, chives and chopped meats are fried quickly on a wok and eaten in your fingers.

One of the most interesting things to see in the market is the area given over to birds. Many of the men, particularly the older generation, are passionate about birds and rear them for their singing and fighting ability. Men bring their pets to the market in bamboo cages, often complete with a fitted cover. Groups sit to discuss the merits of their birds and show them off to their friends, whistling at them to make them sing. There is some buying and selling.

The young Miao girls and women make their way to the stalls that sell a wide range of commercial embroidery silks. There are also rich thick satins and heavy gold paper that is incorporated into their embroideries as well as some patterns. Chemical dyes are on sale and many of the Miao women spin, weave and dye their own cotton cloth. A few embroidered and woven pieces made by the older women are sold to the younger girls to attach to their costumes. You can buy a complete embroidered baby

Textile dyes for sale at Kaili market

carrier. Recently the Miao have started a small stall selling silver rings and earrings that are now fashionable among the Han Chinese. Men and women can be seen bending, shaping, forging and buffing up small items of jewellery.

Stalls selling modern factory-made clothing abound and there are endless supplies of brilliantly coloured track suits and cotton blouses, jackets, shirts and sweaters. You can find more modern tight-fitting Guangzhou jeans at another stall and there is plenty of gaudy children's clothing—a copy of a policeman's outfit including hat seemed particularly popular. Trainers and the more common Chinese cloth shoes are available alongside men's leather shoes and a selection of high-heeled shoes for the girls. The haberdashery stall is popular. Girls spend ages buying ribbons, plastic combs and pretty slides for their hair. Mirrors and make-up are favourite items. The vendors are often very kind to foreigners seen examining the goods with interest and may present them with a small present such as a mirror or railway timetable for the province.

Other stalls sell a range of herbal remedies and there is even a dentist on hand who will extract a particularly bothersome tooth. The display of dead rats is not on sale but to demonstrate the efficacy of the poisons offered. More colourful is the display of red-tipped incense sticks to burn at local shrines, a liberal supply of red paper for good luck posters and plenty of firecrackers. Paper money and incense to burn at funerals is near a shop selling large funeral wreaths made of white tissue paper touched with colour. Bright paper kites are on sale, some of gigantic proportions. Everyone will enjoy the beautiful display of baskets of every shape and size made from plaited bamboo. Sorghum brooms are used with the back bent and one arm behind. There are large pottery jars that shine in the sun, topped with covers so that soy sauce and vinegar can be stored safely.

You could be surprised by a government campaign to encourage the idea of people helping each other. In the 1960s an ordinary soldier called Lei Feng was well-liked in the community for the help he gave to one and all. When he died tragically the government made him a public hero to encourage others to follow his example. Although a 1960s model, the idea has been revitalized and twice a year at the Sunday market, government units set up stalls and perform good deeds. You might see people cutting hair, doctors taking blood pressure, the agricultural college giving advice on insecticides, railway staff helping with timetables and others mending radios and televisions.

Miao village near Taijiang in the spring

Marriage Rites and Wrongs

Among the Miao nearly all the disputes arise on account of their land or their women. They recognise the marriage relation, but do not observe it as strictly as the Chinese. Miao women have more liberty and are more unconventional than Chinese women, and consequently many of their marriages are the result of mutual liking. Not infrequently, however, a girl is practically sold for money to a husband chosen by the parents, and in these cases the result is often disastrous. The young woman will probably run away from her husband's home and continue to meet her lover. If pressure is brought to bear upon her from her parents or parents-in-law, as it generally is, she may return to her husband's home, make herself thoroughly disagreeable, and run away again in a short time. After this has happened repeatedly, the husband in despair tries all he can to find out who is the lover. When he finds this out, he sends an invitation to the lover and to his wife's people to come before the elders of the district and talk over his grievance. Sometimes these discussions last for days. The husband pretends to want his wife back, but as a matter of fact he has had quite enough of her, and really desires to have the money he paid for her returned to him. The wife's father pretends to be very angry, says his daughter was not well treated, that notwithstanding the hard work she had to do and little food she got, she is willing to return, but her husband has never come to his home to fetch her. Note, it is the custom for a husband to make a present to his wife's father on such an occasion.

Many angry words are spoken by the three parties concerned, and after everybody has added his or her word to the discussion, the case may be ended by the elders suggesting that the lover should repay the husband the cost of his wife and marry her himself, and that the husband should take the money and go elsewhere for a wife. If, however, the lover's influence is strong, the elders may decide that the girl go back to her husband, knowing that she will do nothing of the sort, or will not stay with him if she does go back. The case is thus only postponed for another time. We have assisted at some of the discussions of these matrimonial cases and know how hard they are to settle. These daughter-in-law cases are not often brought before the Chinese magistrate, except when they have led to fighting, and as sometimes happens, to serious wounds and homicide.

... A man once explained to me how it happens that they have no written language. He said that many years ago the Miao were living in the neighbourhood of the Chinese, and the Chinese were too crafty for them, so they determined to move westward and live by themselves. At that time they knew a few characters, but evidently knew very little else. After travelling for many days they came to a vast sheet of water, and, having no boats, were unable to proceed. As some of them stood perplexed at the edge of the water, they noticed some water-spiders moving about on the surface of it, and they said one to another, 'If these little things can walk on the water, why cannot we?' Thereupon they tried to walk on the surface of the water, which nearly cost them their lives. Before they managed to get back again on the bank, they swallowed a great deal of water, and with the water they swallowed all the characters they knew, and have been without characters ever since! This may be regarded as an historical romance with a basis of fact. They did move west away from the Chinese, and the sheet of water was doubtless the Tungting Lake. But are we to gather from it that there was a time when they had some characters, but have since forgotten them?

Samuel R Clarke, Among the Tribes in South-west China, *1911*

Embroidery papercut of Miao hero, Zhang Xiu Mei riding a horse

Everyone mills around and part of the fun of a market is watching the different people go by. **Taijiang market**, which operates on a five-day cycle, is similar to Kaili Sunday market as both Han Chinese and ethnic groups attend, as well as young and old dressed in the widest range of fashions. Look at the different designs on the back of the baby carriers, enjoy the pleasure of an old man choosing his favourite tobacco, watch the women gossiping, the vendors haggling and the general care that everyone takes in deciding what he or she is going to purchase. It is interesting to watch the local people buying and selling; there is tremendous verbal bargaining but sometimes more subtle hand signals are used. Shopping is a serious business, money is spent with care and an eye for a bargain.

Duyun

Duyun administrative district covers an area of 2,274 square kilometres (878 square miles) and has a population of 417,100, of whom 60 per cent are ethnic people.

Central Government policy during the 1950s of moving industry away from the east coast of China spurred a gradual development of industry and transportation in the area. Until then, Duyun was a very small town whose only industry was small-scale ramie cloth production. Today there is a growing textile industry based on ramie, wool and cotton; some carpet production; chemical fertilizers; waxed paper; building materials; bridge sections, largely for railways; and an expanding electronics industry notably related to satellites.

Sites In and Around Duyun
■ WENFENG PAGODA
A local scholar designed this 33-metre (108-foot)-high Qing Dynasty (1644–1911) pagoda to protect the Baizi Bridge from flooding and to gain merit for himself and enhance his reputation in the town. The small pond in front of the pagoda was believed to be the home of an evil dragon who caused the river to flood.

■ TEA
Extensive tea plantations outside Duyun are always of interest to the visitor. You can sample local teas at a Tea Ceremony at the Dragon River Hotel in the centre of the town on the banks of the river.

■ ETHNIC VILLAGES
Enjoy walking in this very picturesque area and exploring the many Miao, Bouyei and Shui ethnic villages. The Yanghe and Jichang areas are particularly attractive; you will be warmly welcomed at several villages where you can enjoy the costumes of the

(preceding pages) *Threshing rice near Kaili*

people and discover the traditional textile skills of the Shui and Miao.

DUYUN TO LIBO

One of the least travelled tourist routes is the drive through Dushan, where you can stay overnight, and then on to Libo. It is a beautiful drive and Libo is a very friendly town. The nearby major scenic conservation area, the **Maolan Karst Forest**, covers an area of 130 square kilometres (50 square miles). The karst landforms are cut by beautiful waterfalls. The natural vegetation remains and there are plants that have survived from very early periods, retaining characteristics of plants and trees that are now extinct. There are 500 kinds of arbor tree including the ginkgo and the Chinese tulip tree. This conservation area supports musk deer, rhesus monkey and, it is claimed, tiger, ox, bear and leopard.

Travelling to this area provides you with the opportunity to visit the Yao people with their unique culture and costume. Bouyei groups also live here and produce outstanding weaving using locally grown cotton. You can return to Duyun via Sandu, stopping to visit the Shui people.

Suggested Tour Itineraries

■ ITINERARY ONE

Plan to stay two to three nights in **Kaili**, visiting two contrasting villages. Each village takes about half a day to see properly. A special welcoming ceremony and performance can be arranged. **Matang** is an interesting Gejia village that produces outstanding batik costume. In contrast, **Langde** Miao village is recommended for its silver, embroidered costumes and modern lusheng music and dance performance. On the way to Langde, stop at the large complex of kilns where bricks and tiles are made by hand. Water buffaloes puddle the clay and smoke rises from the numerous kilns. Further on, wooden water wheels raise water from the river to the paddy fields.

Don't miss the Sunday market in Kaili. Peasant women regularly sell their traditional textiles and embroideries outside the Kaili Hotel on this day, but you may also find them there during the week. Many of the women have adapted their textiles to modern purses, jackets and waistcoats. Many festivals are held in the Kaili area in January and February, during the low agricultural season (see page 216).

■ ITINERARY TWO

The adventurous traveller should plan a circular tour around Kaili staying at Chinese-style hotels. From Kaili drive two hours to **Taijiang**, a small town with a 90 per cent Miao population. En route, several Miao villages of wooden houses lie along the

(above) *Spring paddy fields in the valley and on the the terraced hillsides near Kaili are kept flooded for the growing season, intercropped with rape;*
(below) *Mount Yuntai, with its beautiful rounded limestone peaks and natural mixed evergreen and deciduous forest, is an excellent hiking area*

The Han Chinese Celebrate: Two Festivals

The major Han Chinese festival, **New Year** or Spring Festival, is calculated according to the lunar calendar and takes place towards the end of January or in February. The festival is celebrated in both town and countryside, but tradition is stronger and the festival longer in rural areas. On New Year's Eve, firecrackers are set off to scare away evil spirits, exorcise ghosts and suppress demons. Brightly painted posters of guardian gods are pasted on doors and couplets written on red paper decorate door frames—these stay for the rest of the year to bring good luck to each household. Below is an interesting selection of these couplets taken from a village to illustrate the melding of old and new:

> After the hard work the harvest comes in.
> We plough the fields and plant the gold.

> The love given by the Party is as deep as the sea.
> We benefit from the Party's policies,
> We are influenced by the Party's good heart.

> The spring wind brings peace to my family,
> The morning sunshine brings me good luck.

> I cry for my mother.
> We brothers feel heartache because my mother died.
> My mother is so kind that her spirit will go to heaven.

People in the countryside, and some families in the cities, stay up all night on New Year's Eve with the lights on to ensure no evil spirits enter the house. The firecrackers are set off on the stroke of midnight and incense is burnt to welcome the deities back and to pay respects to the ancestors.

On New Year's Day relatives visit each other for a big family festival marked by feasting where among the well-to-do the food is rich and sumptuous. However, the most significant food for rich and poor alike is dumplings, *jiao zi*, that are always eaten on the first day of the New Year. The entire family joins in to make the dumplings on New Year's Eve, giving them the chance to chat and catch up on family news. Wheat or rice flour is mixed with water, flattened into discs and stuffed with chopped pork, vegetables and seasoning. *Jiao zi* can be steamed or cooked in boiling water

and may be stuffed with other items holding symbolic meaning—sugar means a sweet life; a coin, riches throughout the year; peanuts, longevity; dates and chestnuts, having a son early. On this day, everyone wears new clothes and friends and relatives are greeted with wishes for 'greater happiness and long life'. Unmarried youngsters and children are given money wrapped in red paper with which they can buy fruit, sweets or firecrackers. Further visits are made to friends and relatives on the second day of the New Year and married couples in the city visit the wife's home. In the past families would visit their clan temple; these do not exist in the modern-day cities of Guizhou. The third day, traditionally 'the day to send off poverty', is occupied by people staying at home to sweep their houses and burn the rubbish. Young city people consider this day an opportunity to visit friends.

The New Year festival in the city is officially a three-day event unless people work far from home when special arrangements are made. Daily celebrations, including lion dances, operas and fairs, take place in the countryside until the 15th day of the lunar month when New Year culminates in a Lantern Festival during which participants walk in the moonlight with numerous colourful glowing lanterns.

Mid-Autumn or **Moon Festival**, held on the 15th day of the eighth lunar month, is symbolic of family reunion as the moon is brighter and fuller than during any other month. The moon is an emblem of brightness and purity and has been toasted in a poem by the Tang writer, Li Bai (701–762):

I raise my wine cup and ask the Moon to join me in a drink.
Facing my own shadow there are three of us now.

Families gather for the Moon Festival in an outdoor courtyard, difficult in today's cities of high-rise flats, to eat fruit, cooked soy beans, peanuts seasoned with spices, taro, and the all-important moon cake, traditionally cut into a number of slices equal to the number of family members. Little of the traditional ceremony to accompany the Moon Festival, such as prostrating yourself before the moon, survives but the feasting continues. Moon cakes in Guizhou vary enormously due to the fact that the Han Chinese here have migrated from many parts of China. The outer casing is usually a shortcake-like pastry and the filling a mix of ginkgo nuts, bean paste and spiced salt. Other moon cakes are filled with coconut or lotus seed paste, assorted fruit seeds, nuts, egg yolk, chicken, ham, cassia and date palm.

Ancestral altar in a Miao home

river and look particularly beautiful in the early morning light with smoke drifting from under the chimneyless roofs. At sunset they glow golden; this is perhaps the best time to drive to Taijiang. Once there, take a trip to **Fanpai** Miao village. The journey up through the terraced landscape is one of the truly spectacular drives of Guizhou. Local girls put on a highly-skilled dance performance, quite different from the usual Miao dances, having a lively tempo and disco-like movements. One village has won provincial dance awards. The girls still wear hand-woven clothes and indigo dyeing is common in the area.

After staying at Taijiang, drive on via **Tang Long** Miao village, well known for its excellent silversmiths, and spend a night at **Shidong** where peasants usually bring textiles to sell to visitors. It is a short drive from there to **Zhenyuan**, a delightful old town on the Wuyang River, home to Qinglong (Black Dragon) Cave, an outstanding Taoist Buddhist temple complex dating from 1530. Outside the town you can visit Feiyunyan Temple, now a museum displaying ethnic costume. From Zhenyuan, travel upriver by boat through a spectacular limestone gorge to **Shibing**. The trip is best in November—with the harvest now in, little water is used for irrigation and the river is at its fullest. (You can also make this river trip in reverse, from Shibing to Zhenyuan.) Overnight at Shibing.

Hikers can spend several days walking in **Mount Yuntai**, a beautiful karst limestone area with rounded peaks and natural mixed evergreen and deciduous forest. Many well-maintained paths crisscross the area, but you are advised to take a local guide as there are hazards such as snakes and it is easy to get lost. Gaiters should protect your legs.

You can then return to Kaili via **Chonganjiang** where there is a hotel by the riverside on the main road out to Kaili. The view is excellent, the proprietor friendly and the food delicious. From here you can visit Gejia groups. Chonganjiang has an excellent market that operates on a five-day cycle, selling everything from vegetables to silver jewellery. Near Chonganjiang, a swinging bridge dating from 1873 spans the river, constructed of 16 parallel iron chains covered with wooden boards.

Once back in Kaili, visit **Zhouxi**, an area famous for silk weaving and silk felt. If you are then travelling back to Guiyang, stop at **Tonggu**, a small village where local Miao women paint scenes from their daily life in watercolours. They are well worth buying if you enjoy a primitive style.

■ ITINERARY THREE
Adventurous travellers are highly recommended to visit the Dong area from Kaili (see page 201 for a detailed itinerary). If you are interested in the Long March, you can include **Liping** in this itinerary by driving there from **Rongjiang** before continuing on to **Zhaoxing**.

Liping was taken by the Red Army in December 1934. Zhou En Lai chaired a Politburo meeting here on 18 December at a shop belonging to a merchant named Xu, next door to the Lutheran Church. It was here that Mao advocated marching on Zunyi; this was done late in December. By 7 January the Red Army had reached Zunyi, capturing it two days later. A small museum in the town houses old pictures and artefacts from this period. Liping today retains the air of an old traditional town.

■ ITINERARY FOUR
From Guiyang drive to Duyun for two nights. Drive on to Dushan for one night. Spend several days at Libo visiting the Maolan Karst Forest and local Bouyei and Yao villages. Return through Sandu visiting Shui villages. You can travel back to Guiyang or to Kaili from Duyun.

(following pages) *Small Flowery Miao lusheng festival near Nankai*

Southwest Guizhou

The southwest can be divided into the Liupanshui area to the north of the region and the Xingyi district, with Bouyei and Miao autonomous counties, to the south.

This area is only just opening up to tourism—be stoical about hotel conditions and guest houses. It has much to offer those who enjoy superb terraced landscapes and travelling in a countryside that has changed little for hundreds of years. Azaleas abound in this region and look particularly beautiful in the spring. Major attractions of southwest Guizhou include the variety of ethnic people and local village markets.

Liupanshui

Liupanshui is an amalgamation of several towns and rural areas forming a municipality of 9,900 square kilometres (3,800 square miles) with a population of 2.5 million. The three major towns are Liuzhi, Pan Xian and Shuicheng. Liupanshui means 'six plate water'.

The main natural resource is coal—the area is described as a 'sea of coal'—making this one of the most important mining areas in Guizhou. A large proportion of the miners come from northeast China. A wide range of coal types is extracted from adit and tunnel mines and exports, including coke, are made to Hong Kong, Japan, India and the USA. Mines produce 12.9 million tons annually; reserves are estimated at 36 billion tons. Visitors can easily avoid the mining areas although they have their own certain fascination.

A large iron and steel plant was established in 1966 at Shuicheng that supplies southwest China with construction steel and exports to Hong Kong, India and Japan. The rich local reserve of iron ore supplies the plant, which operates in cooperation with German companies and experts. The workforce of 20,000 is drawn from many parts of China. Other mineral deposits in the area form the basis for a metallurgy industry and include lead and zinc. Improved rail and road communications along with a strong power industry will further support the development of Liupanshui.

SITES IN AND AROUND LIUPANSHUI
■ ONE-THOUSAND-GINKGO-TREE VILLAGE
Tuole village, 30 kilometres (19 miles) west of Pan Xian, is surrounded by more than 1,200 ginkgo trees over 500 years old. The ginkgoes look particularly beautiful when they turn yellow in November and the nuts are delicious roasted.

■ TEN-THOUSAND-MU BAMBOO FOREST

Laochang township is set amid a lush bamboo forest, 45 kilometres (28 miles) from Pan Xian, situated at 1,800 metres (5,905 feet) and covering 6,000 hectares (14,826 acres). It is worth a visit for its many rare plants and animals.

■ TORCH FESTIVAL

Liupanshui is inhabited by 200,000 Yi people, half of whom live in a compact community at Pugu, near Pan Xian. Their major festival is the Torch Festival, held on the 24th day of the sixth lunar month.

Entertainments include horse racing, bullfighting, cockfighting and dancing. When night falls, the young gather round bonfires with torches to sing and dance. Locals call this 'basking through the moonlight'.

■ HANDMADE PAPER

Handmade paper is produced south of Liuzhi near the small county town of Langdai. A variety of fibres and leaves are used, including those from apple trees. Paper products include toilet paper, babies' napkins and money that is burned for the dead. The number of villages producing paper has decreased recently with improved communications and readily available commercial paper.

The journey from Liuzhi to Langdai takes you past some wonderful landscapes and interesting rich farming areas on the valley floors.

■ BAWAN BOUYEI AUTONOMOUS TOWNSHIP, LIUZHI DISTRICT

The Dabang River flows through this area and on to Huangguoshu Waterfall. There are many waterfalls here worth the walk and you can arrange to visit nearby Bouyei villages.

The Bouyei **Mid-Seventh Festival** takes place on the 15th day of the seventh lunar month when the people worship their ancestors. They gather on the Dabang River to sing, dance, play the suona horn and lusheng pipes and to enjoy a variety of traditional games.

■ LONGFENG (DRAGON PHOENIX) UNDERGROUND PALACE

Located in the Shuicheng iron and steel complex, this karst cave, 800 metres (2,625 feet) long, has a river flowing through it and can hold up to 1,000 people.

■ NANKAI TOWNSHIP

This area, 45 kilometres (28 miles) north of Shuicheng, is an excellent starting point for visiting Small Flowery Miao villages. A skilled team of dancers perform and play the lusheng pipes particularly well. You will also see Yi people here.

Xingyi

Xingyi is a small developing city, capital of a district with an area of 2,915 square kilometres (1,125 square miles) and a population of 593,400. It borders Yunnan and Guangxi provinces and is close to one of China's largest hydroelectric power stations (Tian Sheng Qiao), built in the 1980s, that will stimulate future industry. There is some gold-mining with substantial reserves, largely undeveloped, a large distillery and a sugar refinery.

Making bricks

Sites In and Around Xingyi

■ XINGYI TOWN
Enjoy wandering around the town to admire the traditional wooden buildings, look in the shops and eat at the local restaurants that have not yet been modernized.

■ THOUSAND PEAK FOREST
The limestone scenery, 5 kilometres (3 miles) from Xingyi, with its massive rolling peaks is absolutely stunning. Don't miss the sun rising and setting behind the peaks. You can climb up for spectacular vistas from several points. Mist in the early mornings and late evenings often swirls around the peaks, reminiscent of traditional Chinese landscape paintings.

■ MALING GORGE
Located northeast of Xingyi County, this gorge with its spectacular views extends for 15 kilometres (9 miles).

■ MUSEUM OF WEDDING MANNERS AND COSTUMES OF THE ETHNIC PEOPLE
This museum, established in an old temple complex at Guhou, is well worth viewing for its high-quality displays.

■ ETHNIC VILLAGES
The tremendous variety of Miao and Bouyei villages in the area offers much of interest, in particular don't miss the Bouyei traditional opera. Xingren, a small town

Bouyei man making paper near Zhenfeng

unaccustomed to tourists, is a very good starting point for visiting the Black Miao. This group, said to have migrated from the southeast, are very skilled at embroidery and weaving and wear stunning silver.

ZHENFENG

This small town, free from major industries, holds a market several times a week. Local people, mostly Bouyei, flock to it dressed in traditional costume, many carrying baskets on shoulder poles. It is an unforgettable experience to wander through the market admiring the costumes and local products. The Bouyei girls are very shy and run away from cameras. Their predominantly white homespun clothes look very clean in contrast to the darker colours of the Miao costumes. Visitors can call in casually at villages and the local Foreign Affairs office can arrange visits. At Aiyu, you will receive a wonderful welcome with firecrackers, a dragon dance and singing and dancing performed by schoolchildren. Local delicacies are served and textile enthusiasts will appreciate the locally-dyed indigo cloth used to make traditional costumes. You can arrange a visit to see paper being handmade at Xiaotun and it is sometimes possible to see local ceramic production, but the trek is difficult in wet weather. There are many outstanding views in the area.

The spectacular **Huajiang** (Flower River) **Gorge** on the Beipan River lies on the way from Zhenfeng to Huangguoshu and Guiyang.

■ HANDMADE PAPER IN THE ZHENFENG AREA

Paper production has always been an important craft in China. In Guizhou, as transportation has always been poor, local craftsmen have had to meet local demands. With improved transport, many craftsmen have been forced to stop producing paper but some small centres still exist that are of great interest. In a remote valley outside Zhenfeng and 20 kilometres (12 miles) away at Xiaotun, paper of various quality is produced. It is used commercially for wrapping banknotes and for daily local needs, but not for art paper.

Bark is stripped off a local tree called a *goushu* tree, for which there is no satisfactory translation. This is done carefully so as not to destroy the tree. The bark is soaked in the river and then in a vat with soda. The fibres are washed to get rid of the soda and then steamed in a kiln on site. This softens the fibre ready for beating into a pulp. Local cacti are soaked for a short time and then added to the pulp to prevent the sheets sticking. Individual craftsmen produce the sheets on simple but exquisite bamboo frames. As each sheet is produced, a tally is kept by moving a bead on a string. Each craftsman is paid according to output. Finally, the paper is dried on a heated wall.

Suggested Tour Itineraries

The main reason for travelling in southwest Guizhou is not to visit the towns and cities but to explore the countryside and gain an insight into the way of life of the people. If you are touring southwest China, it is easy to drive to this area from Kunming in Yunnan Province. Stay overnight at the Stone Forest, 126 kilometres (78 miles) southeast of Kunming, from where it is a day's drive (about eight hours) to Guizhou's nearest major towns, either Xingyi or Pan Xian. Itineraries One and Two can be reversed and you can exit Guizhou via Yunnan Province.

■ ITINERARY ONE
Overnight for one or two nights at Xingyi, Xingren, Zhenfeng, Huangguoshu or Anshun and drive to Guiyang.

■ ITINERARY TWO
Overnight for one or two nights at Pan Xian, Shuicheng, Liuzhi, Huangguoshu or Anshun and drive to Guiyang.

SYMBOLIC MEANINGS IN MIAO TEXTILE DESIGN: THE BENEVOLENT DRAGON

Fu Jen Catholic University Textiles and Clothing Graduate Institute:
Textiles and Clothing Culture Center

The image of the dragon first appeared in the hunting-fishing age; people worshipped nature and explained its wonders through mythology. Thunder and lightning and snakes on the road after a heavy rain invoked fear in the hearts of the Miao people. They attribute this phenomenon in terms of the dragon's supernatural strength. The Miao people believe Chi-Yiou is their ancestor, a military leader fighting against the Yellow Emperor. Dragon patterns are necessary to memorialize him. The Miao dragon is different from the Han dragon. The Han dragon possesses the horns of a deer, thus indicating its longevity; it has an animal's head plus the talons of a falcon— symbols of authority and power. Its golden robe represents its regal glory. The Miao dragon, by contrast, looks friendly and benign, for the Miao believe the dragon is a kindly god who gives blessings to human beings. The *Ying Long Song*, another mythology of the Miao, says that raising pigs without the water dragon is impossible: the pigs will not grow to full size. Without the water dragon raising chickens is impossible for the same reason. The water dragon also blesses the crop field with a bountiful harvest. The auspices of the water dragon will ensure big pigs and big chickens and

Miao embroidery papercuts showing the wide range of dragon motifs

will keep the barns loaded with grain. Because of the dragon, the Miao have plenty to eat and wear; every family becomes rich. It is the dragons who pour down the rains that feed crops, they save heroes who suffer misfortune; they also help the poor obtain treasures. These dragons are not despotic or menacing, but lively and good-natured. For the Miao, dragons are a symbol of the good life.

The shape of the dragon pattern is not fixed like the Han's; to the contrary, it is highly stylized. It may be composed with the head of a cow, the body of a snake, the feet of insects and the tail of a fish. These variations impose startling and colorful images. The basic transformations are as follows:

1) **Buffalo Dragon**: Also called the mountain dragon. The buffalo dragon has a pair of buffalo horns, two large eyes and a serpentine body. It also has a single, fan-shaped scale for a hand appended to the body, plus a cloud-shaped line on both sides of the body which looks like the feet of a centipede. The dragon's tail is a fish tail divided into two sections pointing off into two different directions. These fish tail sections are shaped like clouds or bracken, lending the overall image a curly decorative effect.

2) **Fish Dragon**: Also called the Fish-transformed Dragon. This dragon is given a fat and short body with the tail of a goldfish, a tail that is usually as big as an entire skirt. Its body has hard scales but no feet. Dragons with feet have been influenced by the Han concept.

3) **Snake Dragon**: A brocade dragon without hard scales, fins, a beard, claws or horns is the most basic design. It is subject to change, however. With the addition of deer horns, it becomes the water dragon; with the addition of cow horns it becomes the mountain dragon. The mountain dragon has hard scales and fins and a tail whose initial construction veers toward the inside but then circles around and expands toward the outside. The body always exhibits cloud patterns.

4) **Silkworm Dragon**: This dragon has a short, fat body with a conspicuous leg section and a silkworm's shape. Occasionally it is decorated with cockscomb, flowers, herbs and pomegranates. This can often be seen in the embroidery of the Taigong area.

5) **Centipede Dragon**: The body of this dragon is very thin and its visage is distinguished by many fins and a large beard. The head of the dragon is that of a centipede, though the body is that of a snake. In the Miao creation

story, the centipede is a brother of Jiang-yang and is also transformed into a dog, which some people believe to be the totem of the Miao people. Thus, a combination of the centipede and dragon offers respect to the Miaos' ancestors.

6) **Shrimp Body Dragon**: Also called the Shrimp Dragon. Its shape resembles a silkworm dragon but it is distinguished by its shell-like fins. Its body is smaller than that of the Silkworm Dragon.

7) **Human Head Dragon**: One Miao legend tells of an old man who chose a special burial place because a fortune teller advised him that, if he would be laid to rest in this particular spot, he would transform into a dragon. After he died, his family buried him according to his wishes, but they were too anxious to wait long enough for the transformation to be complete. They prematurely opened the tomb and spied a dragon with the old man's head. The Miao believe that human beings can transform into dragons after they depart; this means reconcilliation with God. Such an event will bring good luck and the blessings of heaven (mother nature) onto the departed's descendants. This transformation signifies the highest state of mind achievable by a human being. The Human Head Dragon pattern has a snake's body and a fish tail in addition to a human head.

8) **Flower Dragon**: This dragon has the body of a snake with a peony flower at its end. One legend claims that people may transform into a flower tree after which they transform again into a dragon. A dragon's body with a flower at the tail symbolizes change.

9) **Leaf-Body Dragon**: This dragon's body is formed by a pair of coupled leaves, often forming a bird-shaped or serpentine body. Sometimes wings are added, creating a noteworthy outline.

10) **Fly Dragon**: This dragon is formed with a silkworm body, a bird body, a shrimp body or the body of a leaf dragon. They also have wings, indicating their ability to fly.

In addition to these dragon patterns, there are other examples. *Ying Long Song* presents twelve different kinds of water dragons and twelve different kinds of land dragons. The shapes are varied, especially at the hands of the Miao women, for the dragon can be potentially transformed into any animal shape. All of them display a simple and graceful sense of beauty. This is extremely popular in Qian Dongnan, where Taijiang county is the most representative of this art.

Bouyei girls at a village near Pan Xian

Black Miao girl with silver headdress, near Xingren

Small Flowery Miao women with hemp batik skirts and embroidered shawls

Northeast Guizhou

Tongren and Zunyi are the two major cities of northeast Guizhou. Chishui lies to the far west of the area on the edge of the Sichuan basin, in marked contrast to the rest of the province both culturally and geographically.

Tongren

Tongren, designated a city and development node in 1987, has reasonable transport links to nearby Hunan and Sichuan provinces. Minor industries associated with building materials and food processing are its economic mainstay.

FANJING MOUNTAIN RESERVE

Tongren's main tourist attraction lies 40 kilometres (25 miles) to its northwest. This mountainous area, rising to 2,494 metres (8,182 feet), was famous for its beautiful scenery during the Ming Dynasty (1368–1644) when a Buddhist retreat and monastery was established on its upper reaches. The monastery was plundered during the Ming and Qing dynasties and again around 1949; it is currently being rebuilt and refurbished with money raised from local donations and tourists. The new interior is very bright and garish and so far there are only one or two monks in residence.

In the 1930s, Chinese and foreign botanists became aware of the importance of this basically uncultivated landmass for its species of plants and trees. In 1978, the Fanjing mountain area was established as a 567 square kilometre (219 square mile)-reserve; by 1981 it was put under the Guizhou Environmental Protection Bureau. At present, only a handful of Chinese and foreigners visit the area but it has enormous potential for nature lovers.

Plant life is distributed vertically from subtropical at the lower levels (500 metres, 1,640 feet) with broad-leaved and bamboo forests, to a temperate evergreen and deciduous belt higher up, making it an important area for botanical research. Particularly beautiful are the dove trees, azaleas and rhododendrons. Over 300 types of fern and an interesting range of flowers grow in the reserve. Among the 167 species of birds, you might spot Mandarin duck and pheasants. Of the mammals, scientists are particularly interested in the golden-haired monkey. Only around 170 of these fabulous monkeys still survive in the wild, all of them living in this relatively small area in southern China. They are now a protected species. Reptiles also play a significant role in the wildlife of the reserve; one to look out for is the giant salamander. The area is gradually being surveyed and is carefully protected as part of the United

Nations Man and Biosphere programme. Prohibitions have been placed on the felling of trees and the destruction of flora and fauna. There are severe punishements for contravening the regulations; recently a farmer received three years imprisonment for capturing a golden-haired monkey. The area is inhabited by only 1,000 people.

The best months to visit are March or April, late September and October. Avoid the rainy season—May to July—when the humidity is extremely high and rain often causes dangerous landslides. This is the season when you are most likely to be bitten by snakes. Particularly poisonous are the local pit vipers; wear gaiters or other protective clothing on your legs at all times.

■ GETTING THERE

Travellers must get permission to visit from the reserve headquarters at Heiwan, from where you will be given directions along the paths. It is possible to get accommodation at the Heiwan guesthouse, though this is largely used by scientists. Take a jeep or hike the 7 kilometres (4.3 miles) up the beautiful valley along a stone and dirt track to the steps to Jinding. It is a long climb up the 7,000 steep stone steps through lush forest that gives way to shrub. For those whose stamina is not up to the climb, you can hire two porters to carry you in a bamboo chair for approximately 250 *yuan* but very steep sections have to be negotiated on foot. The climb gives you beautiful views of mountains mysteriously appearing and disappearing through mist and cloud. There is a hostel in Jinding where you can stay in a dormitory with four to ten beds. The caretaker may be persuaded to cook a basic meal over an open fire outside.

Climb a further 500 steps up past Jinding for spectacular rock formations and to view the peaks. From here you might see the 'Buddha's halo', a rainbow-like effect caused by certain atmospheric conditions that appears over the mountains. An optical illusion allows you to see your own shadow in the ring. Buddhists believe only those who have performed sufficient charitable and pious deeds will see this phenomenon. There is a small Buddhist monastery here that is being rebuilt at which very basic accommodation is available if you wish to stay overnight before beginning your descent the next morning.

To study the flora and fauna in any depth, you will need to stay for an extended period on the mountain. Hotel facilities are being built halfway up Fanjingshan (*shan* meaning 'mountain') above Heiwan. Only the fit should consider this journey.

Zunyi

Set in the 'rice bowl of Guizhou', Zunyi covers 311 square kilometres (120 square miles), including the urban area of 47 square kilometres (18 square miles), and has a

Elusive Monkeys

At five o'clock in the afternoon, when we had climbed to the village of Huixiangping, not far from Golden Summit, we discovered the first traces of the monkeys. Everywhere twigs and leaves were scattered about, and occasionally we saw fresh monkey droppings. My companions informed me that we surely would have seen the golden monkeys if we had arrived the day before.

We continued climbing, finally arriving at our camp-ground—Treasured Rock. We had just finished unpacking our gear when one of the laborers suddenly sang out, 'Magic light! Magic light!' I looked in the direction of Golden Summit and saw a patch of orangy-rose-colored cloud approximately three hundred feet distant. Unfortunately, the magic light was partially hidden by the summit itself and we could not see its beginning. As we were all exhausted from an entire day of climbing, none of us had the energy to climb the next rise, even though it was not very high; we had to place all our hopes on seeing this sight the next morning.

At the foot of the mountain it had been too hot to wear even a jacket, but on top of the mountain we had to put on our padded cotton coats and wrap

A rare golden-haired monkey

The misty, mysterious mountain peaks of Fanjing

up in our quilts. We hastily had something to eat and went straight to bed. The wind was a demon, disturbing our sleep the entire night. It beat on our plastic tarps and lifted our quilts like a hurricane. The cold penetrated to my marrow. Finally the wind blew away our tarps and other protective coverings, and we felt as if we had been abandoned in the path of a glacier. One of the laborers cursed out loud as he pulled his quilt over his head. We had not a minute of sleep all night.

Morning finally came, and we climbed to Golden Summit as we had planned, but the strong wind, cold rain, and dense fog drove away any interest in going farther. We could not even see clearly the famous scenic spots nearby, let along the magic light. Hurriedly we placed our pot over a fire and cooked our meal so that we could get away quickly.

After coming down from Golden Summit, we walked in the mountains for two days, finally arriving in the village of Yanhaoping, 5,478 feet above sea level. Here we had planned to build our station for observing the Guizhou golden monkeys.

In Yanhaoping conditions were a lot better than on Golden Summit. We had a triangular tent and a spring nearby; wind, rain, fog, and humidity were also not so severe as on Golden Summit. One of the laborers returned to the nature reserve offices after he had deposited the luggage, leaving us a 'community' of three. One of us went to collect firewood, one to wash rice, and the third to make chopsticks. We tied wild vines to the trees for a clothesline, and we made a dinner table by placing a woven bamboo mat on a tree stump. Our situation was much like that of Robinson Crusoe, destitute on his desert island. Our soap, toothpaste, and toothbrushes were put beside the spring, and my watch and camera were hung on a tree where only monkeys could reach them. Our daily routine consisted mostly of cooking, talking, and looking for monkeys.

Our tent was hidden in dense forest, the haunt of the Guizhou golden monkeys. On all sides of our tent the forest was so thick with arrow and thorny bamboo that it was very difficult to enter. The tent was also overhung with evergreen and deciduous leaves of the mixed broad-leaf forest. Most of the plants belonged to the Symplocaceae, the Celastraceae, the Fagaceae, and the rose families. This is the normal habitat for Guizhou golden monkeys, since they spend most of their time in the crowns of these big trees. The leaves, buds, bark, and fruit of the trees are their favorite foods.

Each morning after breakfast we all went out to search in the nearby mountains, keeping a sharp look-out for any movements of the monkeys and observing and studying the traces the monkeys left behind.

We stayed in the mountains for five days, with no sign of monkeys. During those five days and nights we were patient but anxious, hopeful but uncertain. The waiting made me feel quite lonely, but our talks around the campfire and the local Guizhou songs soon relieved this feeling. Whenever a stranger comes to the mountains, the people offer him cigarettes and tea. When they meet someone on the road, whether they know him or not, they always greet him and talk with him for a little while. This friendliness has more to do with the natural environment than with civilized society. Comparing the silence and peace here in the mountains with the noise and crowded conditions of the cities, I thought of words spoken by a man of the Guizhou Television Broadcasting Station. He had once stayed in the mountains for three months, and after returning home, he said, 'I seem to have just returned to earth. I want very much to hear people talk.' People love nature, but they do not want to return to a primitive way of life. What many of us are searching for is a kind of harmony between society and nature—a big problem yet to be solved in today's modern world.

Tang Xiyang, *Living Treasures:* An Odyssey through China's Extraordinary Nature Reserves, 1987

population of 435,100. Zunyi lies on the Xiang River, a tributary of the Wu Jiang. It is the administrative and economic centre of north Guizhou and is situated on the main railway line linking the province with Sichuan to the north.

Originally known as Bozho, the Tang poet, Li Bai, called it 'a savage and a waste land'. Today it is a modern city, nicknamed the 'emerald of north Guizhou' and famous for its connection with the Long March. Within the province, Zunyi has the reputation of spawning wiser people than anywhere else in Guizhou.

During the 1930s when the Red Army arrived in Zunyi it was the second largest city in the province. After fleeing their base in Jiangxi Province, hotly pursued by the Nationalist forces, the Red Army fought its way across Hunan and had narrowly escaped defeat by the time it reached Zunyi at the beginning of 1935. The historic Zunyi Conference took place in January of that year at which Mao Ze Dong became de facto commander of the Red Army and member of the Standing Committee of the Politburo. Mao Ze Dong's political and psychological acumen, vividly displayed during the conference, was pivotal in the fortunes of the Red Army and the Communist Party. Mao's guerilla tactics and his conviction that the Nationalists should not, at this time, be engaged in decisive battle were accepted, and his policy of 'going north to fight the Japanese' was adopted. Thus, as the Red Army marched northwest to Yanan (Shaanxi Province) that was to become its base, it was in a spirit of advancing to attack rather than one of retreat.

Traditionally a famous silk spinning and weaving centre, raw silk is still produced in the area. Along with this, some imported silk from the lower Chang Jiang basin is woven. Zunyi is particularly well known for its pure silk duvet covers. Cotton textiles are also manufactured. Another ongoing traditional industry is the production of Maotai and other Chinese wines that are famous throughout China.

Industrial development has been encouraged by the recent hydroelectric power station on the Wu Jiang and other schemes. The city has a growing industrial base including chemicals and plastics, food processing, metallurgy, light engineering, an expanding hi-tech industry, an automobile plant producing trucks and cars and a ferro-

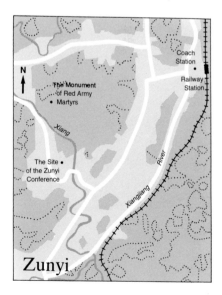

alloy plant. Zunyi's large manganese reserves as well as aluminium, coal, sulphur, mercury, phosphorus and marble will further stimulate industry. Large crops of tobacco are grown in the area and are flue-cured, forming the basis of an important tobacco industry.

Site of the influential Zunyi Meeting, now a museum

SITES IN AND AROUND ZUNYI

The city centre is modern and attractive with tree-lined streets and a number of parks.

■ THE ZUNYI MEETING SITE

The Western-influenced walled house, a former landlord's residence built in 1920, was used by the Red Army leaders. Soldiers assembled in the large courtyard. Bedrooms of the various leaders, including Zhou En Lai, are furnished as they were in the 1930s—a simple wooden trestle for a bed covered with a straw mattress and cotton quilt. Straw sandles and an umbrella from that time are also displayed. Some rooms, including the Conference Room, are set out with the landlord's original luxurious furniture. Rooms were heated by burning charcoal on stones under the table.

■ RED ARMY GENERAL POLITICAL DEPARTMENT SITE

A church and its beautiful house, set in lush grounds and built by the French in 1866, is now an exhibition centre for the Long March. Old photographs and memorabilia are well displayed and lit; worth a visit.

■ MONUMENT OF THE RED ARMY'S MARTYRS

This large monument, built in 1985 and designed by the Sichuan Art Academy, depicts the story of the Long March and the major battles in Guizhou. These enormous sculptures make an interesting contrast to the simple plaque to the Unknown Soldier and the memorial statue to Doctor and Child that lie behind it in a quiet green area.

Huge stone memorial statue to the Red Army martyrs, Zunyi

■ OLD TOWN

It is worth taking some time to walk through the Old Town and to visit the Xianshan Buddhist Temple.

■ WINE FACTORIES

The most famous of these factories making Dong wines is in the north of the city and has won many State awards. Other factories are on the outskirts of the city. The best-known brands are Maotai, Xi, Zheng and Yahan. Note that the Chinese character translates as 'wine' although more correctly these are 'spirits'.

■ MEI TANG TEA GARDEN

You can make a day trip to the Tea Garden, two hours drive from Zunyi in Mei Tang. Contact the Foreign Affairs office in Zunyi or the main CITS offices for advice on arranging a visit. The tea, a local speciality, is called Mei Jiang and is sold at 250 *yuan* for half a kilogram (one pound).

■ LOUSHAN PASS

The importance of this pass, 45 kilometres (28 miles) north of Zunyi through the Dalou mountains, lies in its historical connections. On 27 February 1935, a section of the Red Army wrested the pass from the control of the Nationalist Army and then swept into Zunyi. They took over 2,000 prisoners and captured 1,000 rifles and 100,000 rounds of ammunition. This victory lifted the spirits of the Red Army that had suffered from weeks of double-speed marching and lack of food and sleep. Mao Ze Dong wrote a song to commemorate this event in February 1935:

> Fierce the west wind,
> Wild geese cry under the frosty morning moon.
> Horses' hooves clattering,
> Bugles sobbing low.
>
> Idle boast the strong pass is a wall of iron,
> With firm strides we are crossing its summit.
> We are crossing its summit,
> The rolling hills sea-blue,
> The dying sun blood-red.

■ MAOTAI

Famous for the production of Maotai liquor, a fiery spirit made from sorghum and wheat, this town is located 100 kilometres (62 miles) to the northwest of Zunyi. Maotai, close to pure alcohol, used to be shipped north to Sichuan with cargoes of

The Long Hard March

The stony track leading north through the Taloushan Mountains toward the border of Szechuan was hard with frost beneath Jakob's callused feet, but as he climbed in the gathering dusk at the end of the line of prisoners, the faint, sweet fragrance of winter plum blossom unexpectedly teased his nostrils. In the gloom he could just see the outline of a grove of trees whose bare branches were speckled with the early blossom, and the perfume of the white flowers lifted his flagging spirits. Ahead of him the troops were lighting torches made from bunches of mountain bracken lashed to staves: they flared brightly in the half-darkness, casting a warm glow over the long, winding column of marching men, and spontaneously the soldiers began to sing as they climbed.

A silver crescent moon already lifting into sight above the peak of a distant mountain was spilling cold, pale light on its highest crags and in the dome of the darkening sky a few faint stars were beginning to twinkle. Against Jakob's cheeks the chill night air of the mountains was sharp but there was not a breath of wind and his body was warm inside the quilted long-gown his guards had given him at Tsunyi. He climbed more easily, since the foot lacerations he had suffered at the Hsiang crossing had been given a chance to heal during the twelve-day rest in the old walled city. The constant marching had also at last begun to toughen his feet, making the soles coarse and leathery. The grooves worn in his insteps by the bindings of plaited straw sandals had also ceased to chafe as calluses hardened to form a horny, protective hide inside the flimsy footwear.

As they marched in the stillness of the approaching night, the rough voices of the peasant troops raised in unison carried clearly along the winding tracks, echoing from the funneled walls of ravines and flowing invisibly up and down the bare hillsides of the Taloushan. The singing, Jakob could sense, was binding the column together, fusing the thousands of marchers into one serpentine body, imbuing each man with renewed vigor from a common well of energy. Although he did not join in and the sentiments bellowed into the night were crudely exhortatory, in the deep silence of the mountains the songs in their essence took on the emotional

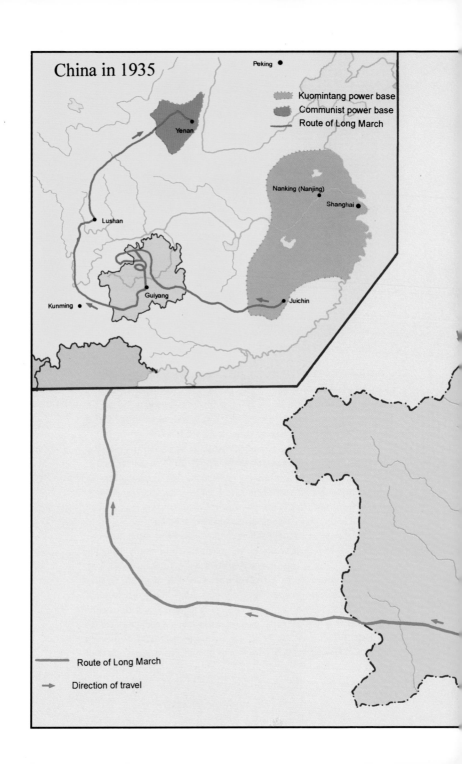

China in 1935

Kuomintang power base
Communist power base
Route of Long March

Peking

Yenan

Nanking (Nanjing)
Shanghai

Lushan

Guiyang

Kunming

Juichin

Route of Long March

Direction of travel

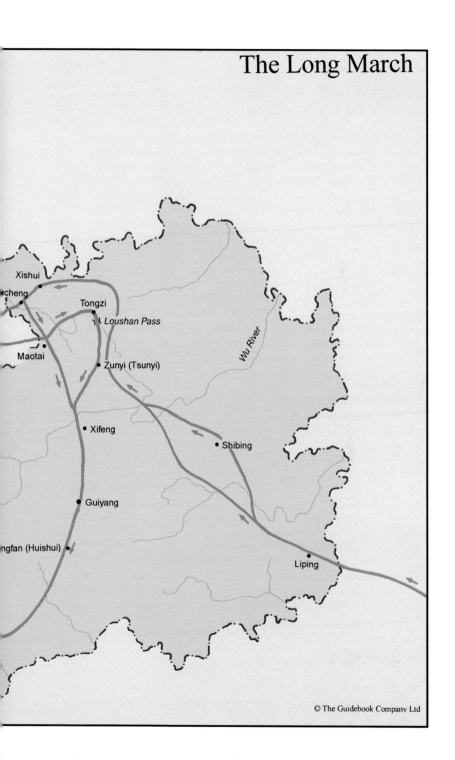

The Long March

Xishui

cheng

Tongzi

Loushan Pass

Wu River

Maotai

Zunyi (Tsunyi)

Xifeng

Shibing

Guiyang

ngfan (Huishui)

Liping

© The Guidebook Company Ltd

force of hymns and Jakob felt himself strangely stirred by them.

Not for the first time, the cadences of the youthful voices inspired in him an illogical feeling of community with the multitude of troops marching all around him. He felt keenly the power of the common loyalty which bound them together; he felt the intense shared excitement of the challenge they faced, fleeing from a superior enemy into an unknown future, every man equal and carrying only the barest essentials for survival on his back—chopsticks, a rice bowl, a quilted blanket, an umbrella of oiled paper, a rifle. Jakob sensed that having survived the fiery slaughter of the Hsiang River, each man felt himself chosen to fight on for his fallen comrades as well as himself and faith in their cause seemed to ring from the soul of every man when they sang on the march. On such occasions the atmosphere of the column was that of a great spiritual crusade in which every individual gloried in the dangers and hardships still to be met. Jakob never forgot for an instant the deep hostility to his own faith that the Communists harbored and he still prayed fiercely each day for help to show them forgiveness for having so callously taken Felicity's life and robbed him of his daughter—but despite all these things, the strange sense of kinship with the soldiers constantly reasserted itself.

On other fine nights since leaving Tsunyi, when enemy regiments were known to be far off, the troops had also lit torches and sung as they marched beneath the starlit heavens. Often snow had dusted the Taloushan, etching its peaks on the sky in bold strokes of light and shadow, and the calm, silent beauty of these night landscapes had then, as now, induced a tangible sense of awe in the marching men. Their moving presence enhanced the scene when the torches they carried spread a rose-colored glow above their bobbing heads and from the heights, the entire column often became visible winding across the darkened highlands like the coils of a long, crimson dragon.

Amid the rough talk of the soldiers Jakob heard no direct reference to the awe-inspiring splendor of their surroundings. Something in their subdued demeanor, however, betrayed an instinctive respect. Whenever Jakob sensed that these unspoken feelings were becoming intense, the men around him invariably burst into their noisy, raucous propaganda songs, as though to prevent their minds from dwelling too deeply on the eerie majesty of the towering crags and black ravines which seemed to dwarf them into insignificance.

'Come, My Friend, We Must Avenge Our Parents' Deaths,' they would roar into the darkness, or they would bellow 'Let No Chinese Fight Chinese!'. . . 'The Red Army Will Surely Be Victorious'. . . 'Someday We Will Fight Our Way Back to Our Native Villages'. . . In one song after another of a repertoire that was becoming familiar to Jakob, accents of all the southern provinces—Kiangsi, Kwangtung, Fukien, Hunan, Kwangsi, Kweichow—blended in ragged chorus. But again and again the marching troops returned to one song above all others, 'Till the Last Man,' and as they climbed they brandished their torches above their heads both to rekindle the flames and to lend added emphasis to their strident rendering of the words:

'The sacred earth and freedom
Who dares to seize them from us?
Our red political power,
Who dares stand in our way?
Our iron fists are ready
To strike down the Kuomintang.'

Many of the troops wounded at the Hsiang River still wore bandages on their heads and limbs: some had lost fingers, hands, or an eye, some had a bandaged cauterized stump in place of an arm, others limped and dragged a shattered leg or foot. Many heads had been shaved to the scalp to rid them of lice, many still suffered from boils and malaria, and dysentery had wasted other bodies and faces. But the wounded, diseased, and healthy alike shouted the songs with equal gusto, buoyed and supported by the intense camaraderie produced by shared suffering and survival against the odds. One company or battalion would take up a song, another would answer with its own version, yelled louder or more lustily, and the valleys and crags echoed and re-echoed with the choruses offered in fierce, friendly competition.

Now that most of the superfluous equipment had been dumped, the transport column marched separately, mainly at night. Even the heavy artillery weapons had been abandoned for lack of ammunition, and sometimes Jakob and the other prisoners walked in the wake of the less encumbered baggage mules, while sometimes they moved more quickly with the fighting columns.

Anthony Grey, Peking, 1988

THE LONG MARCH

The Long March is one of the great epics of history. The Communist Party of China (CCP), formed in the 1920s, initiator of numerous campaigns to raise standards for workers in the eastern cities, committed to 'land to the tiller', peasant literacy and women's rights, had retreated to the remote mountainous areas of Jiangxi Province. Here a disciplined military force was built up on strict puritanical lines. Chiang Kai-shek, leader of the Kuomintang and opposition party, worked to defeat the Red Army of

Mao Ze Dong on his horse, surrounded by Red Army soldiers during the Long March. Yu Youhan, acrylic on canvas, 1993

the CCP by constant attack. In October 1934, the Red Army's decision to slip away with 100,000 men and women began the now famous Long March, a retreat of 9,600 kilometres (5,965 miles) west through Hunan, Guangxi, Guizhou, Yunnan and Sichuan, through high snowy mountains and deep valleys, fighting every inch of the way until a safe base was established at Yanan in Shaanxi Province. Guizhou at the time was incredibly poor, ravaged by feuding warlords and its people stupefied with opium. The Swiss missionary, Alfred Bosshardt, born in Manchester, and his wife, Rose, were captured by Red Army soldiers while working in Guizhou in a Methodist mission. Rose was released but her husband was forced to walk and ride in horrendous conditions with the soldiers through Hunan and Guizhou until he was finally released in Yunnan.

His experiences and life in Guizhou are recorded in his book, *The Guiding Hand*, while his life story has been adapted by Anthony Grey in his exciting fictional book, *Peking*.

opium along the Chishui River. Today the pungent smell of fermenting mash pervades the town as factories stretch all along the river.

Chishui

Chishui, officially designated a city in 1990, lies at an altitude of 280 metres (919 feet) and is surrounded by hills rising to 1,700 metres (5,600 feet). It has earned its nickname, 'pearl of green land', from its vast areas of forest. Chishui, which only became part of Guizhou Province in 1728, is physically, economically, historically and ethnically closer to the red sandstone basin of Sichuan. Chishui River connects with the Chang Jiang (Yangzi) river system, a useful trade route for merchants of old who brought salt along the ancient trackways to send it upriver to Chongqing, 200 kilometres (124 miles) away in Sichuan, where salt was always scarce. Chishui has been earmarked as a site for industrial development, partly because of the continuing advantage of this good river communication with Sichuan.

The subtropical climate gives an average annual temperature of 18°C (64.4°F) with extremes of 41°C (105.8°F) and 2°C (35.6°F). Two crops of rice are grown and mulberry trees are cultivated for the rearing of silkworms. Other main crops are rape, sweet potato, wheat, maize, peanut, soya bean, potato and tobacco. This is a centre for fruit growing, including lychee, longan, orange, banana, pomelo, peach, apple and pear. A variety of vegetables are produced and many peasants now specialize in high-value crops such as a mushroom, *dictyphora indufita*, that grows on the bamboo rhizome. In the hills China fir, camphor and bamboo is felled.

Natural gas in the area is the basis of a large chemical factory that produces synthetic ammonia and urea, employing over 3,000 people with 1,000 living on site. This gas also powers local buses—easily spotted by the large rubber balloon-like covering on the top that holds the natural gas. Good supplies of hydroelectric power have enabled other industries to develop such as high-quality paper production based on bamboo and other woods; shipbuilding, notably river boats for use on the Chang Jiang; light engineering; textiles originally based on silk; and food processing associated with a wide variety of agricultural products. Chishui is also famous for the distillation of Maotai and other liquors. There are a number of traditional bamboo crafts such as flute- and basket-making.

Sites In And Around Chishui
Chishui's beautiful scenery has been described by Chinese scholars as 'one thousand waterfalls competing with each other'. It is linked by river to the heavily populated

Majestic bamboo forest at Jinshagou

areas of Chengdu and Chongqing and has historical connections to the Long March and the dramatic crossing of the Chishui River by the Red Army.

With the new ease of movement inside China, domestic tourism is growing. In 1988, representatives of Central Government in Beijing designated Chishui a tourist development area. With great foresight, the Chishui Government collected 100 *yuan* per head of the population, constructed paths to the scenic areas and built roads. By 1990, Chishui was accepted as a provincial level scenic area and in 1992, Chishui applied for state level scenic area status such as that enjoyed by Huangguoshu.

■ SIDONGGOU

Sidonggou means 'a valley with four openings' and is 17 kilometres (10.5 miles) from Chishui. There is a new stone pathway running through the valley that takes you past four exceptionally beautiful waterfalls of varying heights. The valley is clothed in green bamboo, broad-leafed trees and a large range of ferns, the most famous of which is the tree fern (*alsophila spinulosa*). The surrounding area is crisscrossed by ancient trackways used by traders before the roads were built. It is an excellent walking area, giving you a taste of village life as farmers pass by with their goods on shoulder poles. Interesting traditional Chinese gateways along the way commemorate the traders' wives. One of these was erected to a wife who showed extreme fidelity to her husband by not marrying again, in accordance with ancient Chinese custom, although she was widowed at the age of 14. Carved stone tablets protect the traders on their journey. You can see water-powered grinding mills and paper-making workshops. Old peasants can still recall the passage of the Red Army.

■ SHIZHANGDONG SCENIC AREA

Thirty-seven kilometres (23 miles) from Chishui, along a good road, is the Zhongdong Waterfall on the Fengxi River and beyond is the spectacular Shizhangdong

Waterfall, 80 metres (262 feet) wide and 76 metres (249 feet) in height. You can walk down to the river level and stand behind the roaring curtain of water, then walk along the beautiful green valley that has a wide variety of ferns and other plants. Nearby is 6,000 hectares (14,826 acres) of primeval forest with rare animals and plants. Camellias and azaleas are particularly beautiful in the spring.

■ JINSHAGOU
Jinshagou, meaning 'golden sand', is 40 kilometres (25 miles) from Chishui and is divided into two areas. The first is the Spinulosa Tree Fern Protected Area, extending over 32 square kilometres (12 square miles). This is the first protected area of its kind in China,

Protected tree fern at Sidonggou

gaining its status in 1984. *Alsophila spinulosa* tree ferns, known as living fossils, were the food of dinosaurs 200 million years ago. The fossil evolved in the Jurassic period of the Mesozoic era and is now a rank one protected plant. Other plants of this period have died out and the tree fern remains in only a few parts of China and other areas of the world. It grows well in these valleys in the subtropical conditions below 750 metres (2,460 feet). The area is guarded and only scientists have access for research purposes. Groups can gain permission to enter the area under special circumstances. Convenient paths have been laid out. There is also a wide variety of other ferns, bamboo, trees, plants, insects, reptiles, amphibians, birds and mammals.

The second area, 18,000 hectares (44,479 acres) of bamboo forest, is not classed as a protected zone and is partly open to visitors. One section was planted with bamboo from Fujian Province in the 19th century that now grows to the exclusion of other plants and trees except one or two huge camellias. Artists and those who appreciate Chinese paintings of bamboo will be overwhelmed by this forest. Du Fu (619–907) wrote in a poem that he could live without pork but never without bamboo, for 'no pork makes a man thin, while no bamboo makes a man vulgar'.

■ **DANXIA LANDFORMS**
Giant red sandstone boulders have been carried down the river beds of many of the valleys in the Chishui area. These often give rise to spectacular landforms when perched on top of each other on the hillsides—the Chinese poetically refer to these as 'red clouds'.

Suggested Tour Itineraries

The two tours below each cover a two-to-three week holiday in Guizhou and would be of interest to botanists, walkers and historians.

■ **ITINERARY ONE: BOTANY AND NATURAL HISTORY**
Start in Chongqing, Sichuan Province. Boat all day to Chishui and stay for three nights, bus to Jinshagou (two nights), bus to Zunyi (300 kilometres, 186 miles) (two nights), bus to Guiyang (180 kilometres, 112 miles) (two nights), bus to Tongren (480 kilometres, 298 miles) (one night), bus to Heiwan, base of Fanjing (one night), walk to Jinding summit, stopping one night en route. Return to Heiwan (one night), bus to Tongren (one night), bus to Kaili (one night), bus to Guiyang. An alternative would be to depart Guizhou through Hunan Province.

■ **ITINERARY TWO: LONG MARCH HIGHLIGHTS IN GUIZHOU AND HUNAN**
Start in Nanchang, Hunan Province (one night), bus to Jingganshan (two nights), return to Nanchang (one night), train to Changsha (one night), bus to Shaoshan (one night), bus to Changsha (one night), bus to Zhangjiajie National Forest Park (three nights), bus to Tongren, Guizhou Province (one night), bus to Kaili (280 kilometres, 174 miles) (one night), bus to Guiyang (200 kilometres, 124 miles) (two nights), bus to Zunyi (180 kilometres, 112 miles) (two nights), bus to Xishui (270 kilometres, 168 miles) (one night), bus and boat to Jinshagou (one night), boat to Chishui (one night), boat to Chongqing, Sichuan Province (two nights).

Note: The Guiyang branch of CITS have run an exploratory tour of the entire Long March route through China and should be contacted if you are interested in this tour.

A Jerseyman in Guizhou

Keith Stevens

Three imperial provincial armies, those of Hunan, Guizhou and Sichuan, between 1868 and 1874 fought for some six years to quell a long standing uprising in Guizhou Province of the Miao tribesmen. The battles were bitter and hard won by both sides, with the decimated Miao eventually having to seek peace. The uprising, caused by the migration of Han Chinese displacing the Miao from the fertile valleys, has been described in some detail together with a commentary on the first of the two campaigns that made up the struggle from the viewpoint of a Jerseyman who was the weapons advisor to the commander of the Sichuan Provincial Army. The main fighting took place some 64 kilometres (40 miles) east northeast of Guiyang in the area around Huangping and Chong'an.

William Mesny left Jersey in 1854 running away to sea, and between 1860 when he arrived on the China coast until he died in 1919 he sought his fortune in Shanghai and the Yangtze valley. The remarkable part of his career was his rise from being a foreign advisor with the rank of most junior officer to major general in Guizhou Province, and by the time he was 44 he had been promoted to the brevet rank of lieutenant general. He married twice, both times to Chinese ladies and brought up a son and daughter, returning but once to Europe on what was intended to be a business trip in his mid-thirties.

His anecdotal description in his journal, *Mesny's Chinese Miscellany*, of the Guizhou campaign to suppress the Miao rebels included stories of derring-do, imperial troops scaling the heights to drive the well-dug in Miao rebels from their fortifications, the constant sniping and ambushing of the foot coolie supply convoys leading to chronic food shortages, the lack of cooperation between the provincial forces leading to major defeats at the hands of the Miao, and the rewards for bravery. Some of the horrifying aspects included the frequent deaths from sickness, and the utter disregard for the wellbeing of prisoners by both sides. Neither side took prisoners if they could help it, and even when they did the prisoners were soon disposed of to avoid having to guard and feed them. One particularly gruesome episode ensued when a Miao prince was captured and was ordered to be killed immediately by the Chinese brigade commander, and as times were hard and men hungry, the prisoner's body was ordered to be cut up and eaten by the Chinese soldiers. More to the point, the Jerseyman, William Mesny, appeared to see nothing untoward in this act.

Northwest Guizhou

Large parts of northwest Guizhou have been closed until recently, but some of the less remote areas are now accessible to visitors. Weining and Bijie are the main towns. To the west are the Wumeng Shan, the highest and most remote mountains in Guizhou, rising to nearly 2,900 metres (9,500 feet).

This region of Guizhou is very cold in winter with snow and frost. The soil at these high altitudes of 2,000 metres (6,600 feet) and up is thin and there is is a shortage of water; making a living is extremely hard. Buckwheat and maize are the staple grains as it is almost impossible to grow rice. People here belong to various ethnic groups including the Miao, Hui (Chinese Muslim) and Yi.

The Miao are known locally as Flowery Miao, noted by the missionaries of the late 19th and early 20th centuries as being extremely poor. The Yi, known also as the Nosu, migrated from Sichuan and Yunnan. They were an aggressive and warlike band who took land from the Miao. A certain amount of friction between these two communities still exists today, brought to the surface especially on market days when the men have been drinking. The Muslim Hui live mainly in small towns among the Han Chinese, from whom they are mostly indistinguishable, and are the entrepreneurs and tradespeople. The Miao live in remote mountain villages while the Yi tend to live in isolated farmsteads. Neither the Miao nor the Yi practised footbinding, but you can still see quite a number of older Han Chinese and Hui ethnic women with bound feet.

Weining county remains closed to visitors without special permission; check with the Foreign Affairs office in Guiyang before attempting to visit the region. At present, backpackers are not being encouraged to visit the area.

Weining

Weining has no major sites of interest except the market, held every four or five days, that is full of excitement as the Miao, Yi and Hui people converge to sell their produce. You can get to Weining by road from Shuicheng. The scenery is arid with dry stone walls and large fields. It has a strange, wild appeal. Sheep graze the high plateau. In winter, mists swirl and snow falls but in August it is green. The countryside around Weining is ideal for hiking.

CAO HAI (SEA OF GRASS) NATURE RESERVE
One hour's walk south of Weining at an altitude of 2,172–2,234 metres (7,126–7,329 feet), Cao Hai is a paradise for bird enthusiasts. The best time to visit is between

(Above) *A lone heron surveys the scene at Cao Hai;*
(below) *Cao Hai Nature Reserve*

The 'Dry Men' of Guizhou

Zeng Xianhui had never seen anything like it—the poverty of these mountains. Zeng was a poor peasant from Jiangxi, but as the Red Army began to move into the approaches to Guizhou, it entered regions no longer inhabited by Han—that is, Chinese people like the soldiers. They had come to the land of the Miao, a minority race that antedated the Hans and had been driven into these remote stony hills, there to live lives so poor that women could not emerge from their huts—they had no clothes. They sat huddled in nakedness beside straw cooking fires, with the smoke issuing from a hole in the roof. Girls of seventeen and eighteen worked naked in the fields. Many families had only one pair of trousers to share among three or four adult males. The Miao people were frightened by the Red Army, ran from their huts and hid in the mist of the mountains. To them an army meant robbery, rape, murder, the burning of houses, the theft of rice and millet.

This was opium country. Here, as Peasant Zeng observed, almost everyone of the age of fifteen and above smoked opium. They sat outside their huts puffing their pipes with glazed eyes, men, women, and teenagers. The men and teenagers often wore nothing but loin-cloths, the women not even that. The opium was piled up in brown stacks in the sheds like cow dung put to dry. This was not the country of the placid water buffalo patiently plowing the rice paddies. Here the peasants pulled the wooden plows themselves or depended on bony 'yellow cows'—huangniu as they were called—listless mongrels, sometimes ridden by young girls as they fitfully hauled the plow through gummy mud. Here the poor peasants—and all of them were poor—lived in houses made of mud and lath, with thatched roofs. Better houses were built of dark wood, with gray tile roofs and bird's-wing eaves. Here the cao dui, the haystacks, were cone-shaped like the hats of gnomes, and the camphor trees of Jiangxi gave way to parasol or tung oil trees.

Nothing was so bad as the opium. Guizhou was saturated with it. It deadened, drugged, and immobilized the naked poor and it drenched the local armies. *The warlord troops of Guizhou were known as 'two-gun men'—one was a rifle, the other an opium pipe.*

In the arguments about where the Red Army should go, where its next move should be, opium played a persuasive role. The quality of most regional armies was low, but opium depressed the quality of the Guizhou armies to the depths.

Of Guizhou it was said that there were no three li without a mountain, no three days without rain, no man who possessed three silver dollars. This was almost true. The peasants were not slaves in the legal sense, but in many ways they were worse off than slaves. They owned no land. They were in debt to the landlord from birth to death. There was no escape. They sold their children if anyone would buy them. They smothered or drowned baby girls. That was routine. The boys were killed too, if there was no market for them. The price for children fluctuated. In 1983 an overseas Chinese who had been born in Guizhou came back to his native place. He had been sold as a seven-year-old to a middleman for five silver dollars, a very good price. The middleman exported him to Hongkong, where he was resold for four times as much. Eventually he escaped and made his way to the United States; he returned to Guiyang at the age of seventy-five.

The infant mortality rate in Guizhou in 1934 was about 50 percent. It was so high that a child's birth was not celebrated until it was at least a month old. Life expectancy was about thirty years. Poverty was so intense there was little difference between a landlord and a peasant, at least among the minority people like the Miao and the Dong. Illiteracy was total.

Zhu De kept a notebook in which he jotted down impressions of the countryside. Of Guizhou he noted:

'Corn with bits of cabbage, chief food of people. Peasants too poor to eat rice.... Peasants call selves 'dry men'—sucked dry of everything.... Three kinds of salt: white for the rich; brown for the middle classes; black salt residue for the masses.... Poor hovels with black rotting thatch roofs everywhere. Small doors of cornstalks and bamboo.... Have seen no quilts

> *except in landlord houses in city.... People digging rotten rice from ground under landlord's old granary. Monks call this 'holy rice'—gifts from Heaven to the poor.'*
>
> *The poverty of the Guizhou countryside made problems for Peasant Zeng Xianhui. Among his jobs as a cadre was to oversee the expropriation of rich landlords and wealthy peasants. He didn't find many in eastern Guizhou and the Red Army had strict regulations about minority people. They were to be handled with kid gloves because they had been subjected to such exploitation by Han landlords. Peasant Zeng's mind in 1984 still held images of people huddled half-naked in rags along the roads and of passing out clothing he had confiscated from the few landlords. As for opium, Peasant Zeng remembered opening up the barns where the opium balls were kept and inviting the people to come and take it. The Army had no need of opium, Zeng said. Zeng's recollection may not be entirely precise. Opium in this backward land was wealth. Other Red Army men recalled using opium as currency to buy supplies. It commonly circulated in Guizhou as a substitute for money. Peasant Zeng was firm in his memory that the Red Army did not destroy opium. 'We opened the landlords' warehouses and invited the peasants to take it on the grounds that it was produced by their sweat and their labor and belonged to them,' he said.*
>
> Harrison E Salisbury, The Long March, 1985

November and March when the birds are overwintering. The 120 hectare (297 acre) freshwater lake is surrounded by an expanse of marsh and wet grassland within the Chang Jiang river drainage basin.

During the Cultural Revolution (1966–76) the wetland was drained and converted to agricultural land. By the late 1970s, Cao Hai's importance as a wintering reserve for birds—among them cranes, stork, ducks, coot, geese, heron, grebe and spoonbill—took precedence and some of the wetland was returned to its natural state. Over 140 species of bird have been recorded in the area. Protective policies, including a ban on hunting and on the erection of farm buildings, have led to an encouraging increase in the crane population from 35 in 1970 to 350 in 1985/6. Numbers continue to rise. Cranes arrive in late October and leave mid-March. One of the most interesting is the black-necked crane. Jim Harris, writing in the *International Crane Foundation Newsletter*, May 1991, reports:

Azalea in bloom in the spring

Wild azalea on the slopes of Mount Fanjing

Cao Hai has an odd feeling because the cranes are tame, a dramatic contrast to the rest of China. I approached within nine yards of black-necked cranes foraging in a potato field. Here agriculture reaches far into the wetlands, and the birds move among the people on the farmlands. There is a dreamy quality to Cao Hai—birds and people in harmony.

■ GETTING TO CAO HAI
You can make arrangements to visit Cao Hai through GZOTC in Guiyang, CITS or at the local Foreign Affairs office in Shuicheng.

ETHNIC VILLAGES

You can visit Big Flowery Miao and Yi villages in the Weining area, but arrangements must be made through the tourist organizations. Many of the local markets are exciting places to visit. Crowds gather quickly around foreigners—since the departure of the missionaries in 1949, the people of this area have had little or no contact with 'outsiders'. Heavy drinking is a problem in the villages; take note that because of this, people can occasionally be hostile. You will often see groups of men squatting and drinking together, dressed in great felt capes. The atmosphere is suggestive of the early days of the American Wild West.

Bijie And Dafang

The area that includes the two towns of Bijie and Dafang is only just opening to travellers and has not been visited by the author. Dafang is renowned for its beautiful lacquerware. Visit the area in the spring to see the azaleas and rhododendrons.

ONE-HUNDRED-LI AZALEA BELT

Located between Jinpo and Pudi, this area, 1–4 kilometres (0.6–2.5 miles) wide and 50 kilometres (31 miles) long, contains most of Guizhou's 70 varieties of wild azalea. A magnificent azalea festival is held each spring.

Samuel Pollard: A Man with a Mission

Samuel Pollard, at the age of 23, went to China in 1888 as a Methodist minister in the tradition of John Wesley. He worked in northeast Yunnan and, on his numerous evangelizing travels into the countryside around Zhaotong, became interested in a tribal group known as the Hua Miao (Big Flowery Miao). They were extremely poor and oppressed by landlords, often of the powerful Nosu (Yi) group. These Miao were animists whose lives were controlled by wizards, known today as shaman. They were illiterate with no written language and were considered by the missionaries to be immoral, licentious and drunkards. Like the majority of the populace, the Big Flowery Miao were opium smokers.

Pollard built a mission near Weining in Guizhou, in the heartland of the Miao, called *Shihmenkan*, which translates as Stone Gateway. From here he travelled among the people and, before his death from typhoid in 1915, he estimated that there were 10,000 Christians. Of these, 4,800 were trained, baptised and partook of the Sacrament. This was an amazing conversion success story. The Miao were drawn to Pollard and the Christian church as it gave them the self-respect lacking in their lives that were so oppressed by the Han Chinese and the Nosu. Pollard recounts one legend telling of the division of land between the Han Chinese, the Nosu and the Miao. In this legend, the Han Chinese and the Nosu marked their land with boundary stones while the Miao used tied grass. The Han and Nosu plotted to oust the Miao by burning the land, thus destroying the Miao boundary markers and leaving them without definable land.

The church taught the Miao to read their own language using the script that Samuel Pollard had created. Then as now the Miao saw education as a way forward and as a means for changing their circumstances. In his diary, *Eyes of the Earth*, Pollard describes the everyday life of the people and, as well as discussing the number of conversions, he tells of the smallpox, leprosy and typhoid that plagued the population and of the dreadful addiction to opium that was grown everywhere. Pollard regularly describes visits to opium addicts who had attempted suicide. He notes how mothers blew opium smoke across their children's faces in the belief that it would make them stronger and that children were also encouraged to smoke. Opium was cheaper than gambling, a major habit among the Han Chinese and

Miao, which drained families of any monetary resources they might have. He describes the abject poverty of the people and in contrast, the region's rich fauna and flora that included wild boar, wolves and a tiger that bothered the locals in the area of his ministry.

A group of Miao women stripping hemp to make yarn, early in the century

The Miao and Gejia

The Miao is the second largest ethnic group in southwest China and the largest in Guizhou. They live in most regions of the province but there are major concentrations in the southeast, southwest, northwest and in the central area. The 1990 national census put the total Miao population at more than seven million spread throughout seven provinces; half this total is found in Guizhou.

The Gejia people, until 1993 when they gained recognition as an independent ethnic group, were classified as a subgroup of the Miao and for the purposes of this book are discussed together with the Miao, with whom they share a great many similarities.

Origins And History

The origins of the Miao are very uncertain leading to numerous theories among Miao and Chinese scholars. Various conjectures put their original homeland as Mongolia, Tibet or even Lapland but it is generally believed that they were living in the valleys of the Huang He (Yellow River) 4,500 years ago. Some authorities believe they were the earliest agriculturalists in the Huang He valley who terraced the land to grow rice. One theory suggests they were defeated in battle by Chinese tribes and fled south to the middle reaches of the Chang Jiang (Yangzi River) between Lake Dongting in Hunan Province and Poyang Lake in Jiangxi Province. Estimates of how long they have lived in this area range between 2,000 and 4,000 years. It is likely that the Miao migrated to Guizhou in waves from at least the Qin and Han period (221 BC–AD 220). There are definite references in Chinese documents to the Miao living in southeast Guizhou in the Tang (618–907) and Song (960–1279) periods.

During the Song and Ming period (1368–1644) the Miao were under pressure from advancing Han Chinese troops and settlers. Some scholars suggest that it was only at this point that they moved to western Guizhou along the mountains and changed to a slash and burn agriculture from the paddy rice economy that had been based in the valleys and lower hillsides. Others believe that they had already arrived in Yunnan by the ninth century and maintained a presence in west Hunan, Guizhou and south Sichuan. By the Ming and Qing dynasties (1644–1911) the Miao had reached Vietnam, Cambodia and Thailand. After the Vietnam war (1959–1976) the Hmong, as the Miao are known internationally, who had helped the Americans in Laos, were permitted to settle in the US. Today 85 per cent of these resettled people live in California, Minnesota and Wisconsin and some have found new homes in France and Australia.

Historically, the Miao of Guizhou have resented the Han Chinese for levying high taxes on their land. They value personal freedom and have rebelled against oppression. The biggest and bloodiest of the many uprisings against Han Chinese rulers was between 1851 and 1874, led by Zhang Xiu Mei who eventually lost the unequal struggle. Oppression continued, not only by the Han Chinese, but in the northwest by the Nosu (Yi) who treated the Miao as slaves. It is said that Yi and Han Chinese landowners mounted their horses from the back of a stooping Miao.

Linguistically they belong to the Miao-Yao branch of the Sino-Tibetan group. In the early 20th century many Miao were converted to Christianity by missionaries from the China Inland Mission, based in the southeast and at Guiyang and Anshun, and by Methodists from the United Methodist Mission, based in the northwest. Because Miao was not a written language, the missionaries transcribed it in the Roman alphabet and used this to teach the locals to read hymns and the Bible. Samuel Pollard, a Methodist missionary who worked in northwest Guizhou, created his own script for the Big Flowery Miao. Later mission schools were established in the Weining area and arrangements were made for Miao to study at a university in Chengdu. The students who graduated became leaders of the community, which now realized the importance of education. In the 1950s the Han Chinese transcribed the Miao language in Pinyin, however this has proved unsatisfactory due to the number of dialects that cannot be understood by other Miao groups in different parts of Guizhou. Miao authorities recognize four major dialects: western Hunan, southeast Guizhou, southeast Yunnan and southwest Sichuan. Academics are discussing the introduction of a script based on ideographic Chinese characters to allow all Miao to understand each other's writing. As the Miao language, like the Chinese, is syllabic and without conjugations, representing Miao words in this form could work well. Chinese is the official medium of education in schools today, but there have been recent attempts to teach Miao using the Roman alphabet. Many also speak the language of other ethnic groups in their area. Japanese professors are currently studying Miao customs, language and origins in great depth as they believe they may have ancestors in common, although this theory is not generally accepted by the Miao.

An active Communist Party, the introduction of electricity to many rural areas, ownership of TV and radio and an increasing transport network has meant more Miao villages have come into contact with urban society and consumer products. The new Family Responsibility System and the opportunity for development of small enterprises has allowed many Miao to earn surplus cash. Many travel to work in the cities. Some men, for example, work in small private coal mines while others become itinerant workers. Farming is no longer the mainstay of the economy. In the newly developing society, there has been a change in the status of women. In the predominantly agricultural society, men and women were relatively equal sharing farming

(clockwise) Miao girl with silver horn headdress, Duyun area; Miao girl with plastic hair accessories, Taijiang area; Tall-Pointed Hat Miao man dressed for a festival; Gejia baby protected by her silver hat

tasks but since moving to the towns for work, women have become exploited with lower wages. Sadly, the old crafts and skills will begin to die as they become less valued in a society where money takes on an increasing importance.

Classification

Travelling in Guizhou, you will recognize many different groups of Miao, each having distinct costumes, dialects and customs in different regions. Local Han Chinese have given them names that are usually descriptive of and related to the women's dress or hairstyle. Thus there are Black, Red and White Miao, Cock Miao describing the shape of the headdress, Sidecomb because of the position of the hair comb, and so on. They can also be named according to where they live, hence Mountain or River Miao, or by the skirts they wear, Long or Short Skirt Miao. Chinese, European and Japanese ethnologists have tried to classify the Miao using some of these criteria. The Qing text, *Pictures and Accounts of the Miao of Guizhou*, lists 82 categories of Miao but this work also includes other minorities.

At the beginning of the 20th century the Japanese anthropologist, Torii Ryuzo, devised a new system of classification. He recorded five main groups—White, Black, Red, Flowery and Blue Miao—along with a number of subgroups of these main divisions. The most recently published attempt at classification, *Clothing and Ornaments of China's Miao People*, classifies the Miao according to the area in which they live. Miao scholars believe they should be classified more scientifically and according to the name they give themselves in their own language.

Creation Story

The origins of the Miao is steeped in mythology—a particularly colourful story is found in southeast Guizhou where legend says the Miao originated from the eggs of a butterfly. The butterfly emerged from a maple tree; consequently, this tree is sacred and cannot be cut down. The story tells how a bubble and the butterfly married. The butterfly laid twelve eggs that were looked after by a *jiyu*, a mythical bird, until they hatched after many years. Finally, the eggs gave life to a water buffalo, a Miao man called Jiang Yang, a dragon, a snake, an elephant, a tiger and a thunder god, as well as abstract phenomena like disasters, calamities and ghosts.

The memory of the butterfly, the *jiyu* bird and the other animals is kept alive in Miao embroidery designs, particularly among those of the Miao of the Qingshui River in the southeast. Some say as the Miao migrated westwards, the story was lost, others believe the motifs were simplified into geometric patterns. Whichever, Miao groups not living in southeast Guizhou do not know this story, neither is there mention of it among the Hmong of Thailand.

Village Life

The Miao of Guizhou are organized into about 20 overall clans through the male line, each of which has its own name, not often referred to as each Miao will also have a name given at birth. These given names, if necessary, can be changed to overcome misfortune. A strict taboo in Miao society is intermarriage within a clan—a woman, who before marriage will be part of her father's clan, will take on her husband's clan name. The Miao live in nuclear villages made up of several clans with a number of lineages being embraced by each, some in the river valleys but the majority in the mountains.

In the past, the mountain Miao relied on subsistence farming based on slash and burn. After each tree was cut down and burned, and before the rainy season, six to eight rice seeds were planted in the ashes of each hole with the help of a dibble stick. Some barley and buckwheat was also grown. Slash and burn has now largely disappeared except in remote areas to the west of the province.

Both the Miao and the Han Chinese in Guizhou grew opium poppies in the past, often using its leaves as a vegetable. It was planted in the paddy fields after the rice harvest in the 11th or 12th lunar month and harvested before the next rice crop was planted. In the poorer western mountain areas, opium was planted after the maize harvest. The disadvantage of opium is that it takes fertility from the soil. Opium was an important cash crop—families grew it so they could afford to buy silver ornaments for the bride price—and although banned by the Kuomintang Government, it was not successfully abolished until the 1950s. Pollard wrote, 'the fields in the plain now present a lovely appearance. A beautiful white cloak over them all. White poppies! The devil in angel's garb.' Rape and tobacco have replaced opium as the new cash crops.

Village life in the province today varies with the physical attributes of the area. Small gardens with chillies, tomatoes, gourds and vegetables are usually planted near each family house. Paddy rice is grown as a staple in the valleys and double-cropped with wheat or rape. The latter enriches the soil and is particularly favoured. Maize, millet, buckwheat, potatoes and a little sorghum are grown on the high terraced hillsides along with soy beans and other legumes. Maize, indigenous to South America and introduced in the 16th century, is a major crop. It is also used as pig fodder and is dried in the rafters of houses to be used throughout the year. It matures at the

Sorghum and millet out to dry

end of the rainy season while rice matures later, allowing for two crops and thus protecting people from possible famine. The Miao prefer rice, but because of their poverty, often have to eat the cheaper maize on its own or mixed with rice. The Miao also grow rice on terraces high up in mountain areas using a complicated and sophisticated system of wooden pipes to channel mountain streams to the fields for irrigation. Waterwheels are used in some areas for raising water to the terraces and for milling.

Steamed paddy rice is eaten daily by the more prosperous communities. Glutinous rice, which is highly prized and is used for festivals or special occasions, needs more water for its production and is more expensive. Sometimes it is steamed inside banana leaves in small hand-tied packages and given as a snack to guests who unwrap the parcel and dip the rice in honey or sugar. It can also be steamed, pounded in a trough and the sticky dough eaten with sesame powder. This mixture can be rolled out, left to dry and deep fried into crispy rice sheets that are particularly delicious. A red variety of rice is also grown that is sometimes eaten at festivals. Visitors are often offered glutinous rice.

Fish, an important source of protein for the Miao, is stocked in the paddy fields. Traditionally, a poisonous plant extract was placed in the rivers to stun the fish so they could be caught easily. The Miao have been known to use gunpowder and insecticide to kill the fish—this is gradually being stamped out. Chicken and pork are another protein source, eaten intermittently and sparingly at everyday meals, but in larger quantities at festivals. Pigs and water buffalo are well-housed and chickens scratch around for food scraps. Chickens are kept for sacrifice as well as for their eggs, though poultry sold at the market also provides the family with a small income to buy clothes and other manufactured goods. Dogs are important for guarding the household. Horses are used as pack animals. Sheep and goats are kept by some Miao groups in remote mountainous areas and are taken out daily from their pens so they do not destroy the crops.

The men do the heavy ploughing, with water buffalo or oxen; the women transplant rice and help with the harvest. Men perform construction work and the women do the household chores, spin, weave, embroider or produce batik to embellish their garments. Both look after the animals but there is a tendency for the women to look after the chicken and pigs.

Different house styles have developed in the province depending on the availability of building material. You will see houses made of wood or stone, others, timber-framed with wattle and daub walls. Roofing materials vary enormously. In the past, houses were thatched with straw or bark but increasing prosperity has meant kiln-baked tiles are now common. The Miao are particularly well known for their stilt houses built into a natural slope. The Taijiang area is typical of this style. Homes are usually two to four storeys, the animals are sheltered under the house and rafters are used for drying maize, chillies and so on. They are relatively big and spacious but, being constructed of wood, have the disadvantage of burning easily.

Most homes have two hearths and no chimney, hence it is often very smoky. Pig food is usually simmering on one hearth. The floor is packed earth and in the older houses there are no windows or interior doors. There is often a separate storeroom for unhusked rice but there is no protection against rats. Baskets, gourds used as spoons and agricultural implements hang everywhere. A smoked hock of pork might hang from the rafters. Traditionally the ancestors' altar is on the wall opposite the door. Rice, fish tails, chicken feathers and buffalo horns are placed on the shrine to ward off evil spirits, particularly at festival times. Today photographs of political leaders hang alongside those of the ancestors and the family. There is usually a separate room for sleeping. Children move into their own sleeping quarters when they are about ten years old; at puberty they are separated according to sex. Sleeping platforms are being replaced with beds in the wealthier families.

Preparing glutinous rice

During the Cultural Revolution, it was not possible to wear jewellery and it was often buried to keep it safe. Now, the space below the bed is used to store jewellery along with individual clothes. Wooden chests rather than cupboards tend to be used for storage.

For meals, a low table is set up near the fire and people squat on low stools. The family eat together but on special occasions women will eat after the men have finished. This custom is gradually changing. Men often cook for festival occasions. Some villages now have electric lights, TV and radio. At the end of the day when work is over, women sew outside and men chat and smoke cigarettes.

A new house is built when the extended family gets too large. One son and his family stay at home to look after the parents. The older son often builds a new house. Various religious ceremonies and certain rules must be followed to ensure it is a propitious site and that the spirits are not displeased. A new house cannot be directly in front of or behind another—this is to avoid confusion on the part of their ancestors' spirits, who travel in straight lines, when searching for home, otherwise they might enter a neighbour's house. The entire family and their neighbours help to build the house and a feast is given on completion.

Each village will have a village chief who is consulted on everyday affairs concerning social mores. A chief is chosen by the villagers for his knowledge of local customs and is always a well-respected member of the community. He is expected to settle any village dispute between different clans, quarrels between newly weds and to ensure ritual obligations are fulfilled wherever possible. The Miao are generally honest, tolerant and generous. Theft and violence are extremely rare; sources of conflict are usually over adultery or land rights. Today there is also a Party official who must be consulted.

As well as the village chief, a unifying factor is the family whose lineage can be traced through the male line to a common ancestor. Members of the same lineage, added to by birth and marriage, generally live in one village but can get dispersed. All members gather together for important social occasions such as a wedding or funeral. The most respected elder heads the lineage that will always provide hospitality and help to its members.

Most villages today have a school. The majority of children from 6 to 12 years attend junior school, 50 per cent attend lower middle school and a smaller percentage attend senior middle school. The age range for middle schools, which are situated in the towns, is 12 to 18 years.

Girls often do not attend school at all in poorer areas and there are few girls in middle school. It is quite difficult for country children to go on to higher education but a lower pass level is accepted by colleges and universities for those belonging to the ethnic groups.

Religious Beliefs And Funerals

The Miao are animist and shamanist, believing the world to be inhabited by good and evil spirits. Various rituals exist to defend against the bad spirits and ghosts—a protective shrine of phallic stones might be set up near the entrance to a village, or streamers of white paper will be bundled together and placed over the door or on field boundaries. Herbs and mirrors hang from doorways and women often keep parcels of herbs for the same reason. Springs are decorated with cutout paper flowers to pay homage to the water spirits.

In each village there are possibly two shamans with esoteric knowledge to control and communicate with the spirits of the supernatural world. The shaman is called in to help the sick, to perform exorcisms and to officiate at funerals. It is not particularly profitable work and he will always have another job. Shamanism was banned during the Cultural Revolution but probably continued secretly as did other religious practices in remote areas.

Protective herbs and the blood of sacrificed animals—mixed with alcohol and painted over the doorstep—act to deter ghosts. Unless the ghost is particularly harmful or the family involved is wealthy when a water buffalo might be slaughtered, sacrifices are of chickens, pigs or dogs. After the ritual, the family will invite the shaman to feast on the animal with them as part-payment for his services. A second type of shaman who is often approached to heal the sick will work in a trance state.

Glutinous rice is believed to have certain magical powers. It brings good luck to a pregnant woman; she spreads the dry grains on her bed to ensure health for herself and her unborn child. When a baby first walks rice is sprinkled on his hat. If a child is ill, the shaman will be sent for and will hang two rice leaves on a bamboo pole over the bed to encourage the soul to return to the child's body. Parents give rice to their daughter when she marries as a blessing. The fields must be blessed before rice can be planted and, during the seventh lunar month, a ceremony is held to placate the god of the paddy fields during which the shaman will put rice into his mouth before going into a trance state.

Shamans sometimes officiate at fertility festivals. During one such occasion at Langde, Taijiang County, the shaman was dressed in a black costume, a cape of coloured ribbons and a silk hat with hemp tassel. He carried an iron rattle that was used to disperse the spirits. He recounted how, while he was very ill in his twenties, he had been given a vision from the spirit world and had been promised a recovery should he agree to help others during his life. He did recover, and found he was able to make contact with the spirits at will. He became the accepted village shaman and is often asked to protect the children, for which he has designed a papercut motif. He also tells people's fortunes and heals the sick.

Rice and paper charm

Funeral customs vary between regions. In southeast Guizhou, in the Qingshui River area, the bereaved family announces the death to the village by setting alight firecrackers and the relatives are sent for. The body is dressed, traditionally in special clothes made in advance for this occasion. Although an increasing number of people are buried in everyday clothes, women have been found making their own funeral costume even in areas influenced by urban life. A wealthy man is dressed in fine silk clothes and a woman in her best festival costume. A woman's jacket will be buttoned right over left, the opposite to that in life, similarly a man's turban will be wound in the opposite direction. The coffin is laid out in the front room or on a wooden structure in front of the house. Then and at burial it must always be at right angles to the house. Funerals can be costly affairs—a pig may be killed on each day of the funeral for guests to feast on and this can last for up to nine days, depending on the wealth of the deceased. The shaman will spend at least two days officiating at the house to guide the departed to their ancestors. A Miao has three souls, each will go to a different place after death. The first goes to the grave with the dead body; the second, if death has come from old age, will return to the village to help the family. If death has come through accident or disease, however, the second soul will wander the village as a ghost causing problems. The third soul, if the person has died in good circumstances, will return to the ancestors. It is this third soul that the shaman helps liberate. He sings detailed instructions in a long lament on the route to the ancestral home of the Miao, the Huang He or the moon, where there is a good life. These songs are a very important part of the Miao oral tradition. A pair of shoes is placed inside the coffin to help the dead get to their destination.

The body must be buried on an auspicious day. This is variously considered the third, fifth or seventh day after death. The day of burial is accompanied by much feasting and drinking. Lusheng pipes are played and the performers dance in a restrained manner to show respect for the dead person, but as the coffin is lowered into the ground they often leap over the grave. The head must not face east or it will be blinded by the sun and the sons and daughters will suffer misfortune. This is also a Chinese custom. A Miao woman when asked what would happen to her on death said, 'I shall go and visit my ancestors'. These traditional beliefs are not held by everyone today. In common with Han Chinese traditions, grave sites are chosen carefully using the rules of geomancy and are marked by tombstones engraved with the date of burial.

A cremation or a different ceremony will be arranged by the shaman for children, women who die in childbirth or those who die in accidents. The first two souls are released and the second is considered more likely to become a ghost. However, the shaman will give no instruction to the third soul on how to get to the homeland as it is believed this soul will become an evil spirit.

Festivals

Festivals are for fun and their main function is for young people to meet each other and find a marriage partner. Nearby villages usually hold the same festival a few days apart so that everyone can attend each other's. Festivals provide the opportunity to travel around, socialize, meet friends and kinsfolk and be entertained by singing and dancing, water buffalo fights, cockfighting and horse racing. A market is frequently set up during these events that allows people to buy much needed goods.

The Miao are renowned for their dancing, usually performed by the girls to tunes played on bamboo **lusheng pipes** and drums. *Lusheng* is a Chinese name for the Miao bamboo pipe and translates as 'reed instrument'. These pipes are most commonly played at festivals related to courtship and are not generally used at religious gatherings. In the past, lusheng pipes were played only by men and boys and only after the rice harvest, in the belief that a disaster would occur should they be played while the rice was in the fields. Today, girls enjoy playing the lusheng pipes and they are played while the rice is still growing. They vary in size and can be as

Lusheng pipe-playing at Langde

tall as 3.5 metres (11.5 feet). Competitions are arranged to show off the players' skill as they simultaneously perform acrobatic movements or dance with high kicks and spins. These moves have symbolic names such as 'earthworm rolling on the sand', 'dragon rolling on the ground' and 'cockfight'. Players in southeast Guizhou humorously imitate the movement and postures of birds and animals. 'Drinking wine with special skill' is a complicated performance when the player dances around a bench on which a bowl of rice wine is placed for him to drink while still playing. Competitions are extremely popular and hundreds of people gather from participating villages. Winners are chosen for their acrobatic dancing skills as well as for being able to play a number of melodies. **Mangtong pipes**, or base lusheng pipes with a booming tone, are also played by men and women. Slow dances are performed to this instrument accompanied by a **bronze drum**.

The Miao are musical people and most have good voices. There are set songs for courtship and certain rituals. Music, whether sung or played on instruments such as mouth organs, drums, pipes or jew's-harp conveys information to the Miao listener who learns to interpret sounds in the same way as you read a book.

Festivals are concentrated in the low work season from the end of October to April. Weddings are also held in this season and particularly around November, a special month in the Miao calendar. The Chinese lunar calendar, which has replaced the original ten-month Miao calendar, is used to determine festival dates. Organizers must select not only the same lunar month for each annual festival, but must ensure it falls on one of the lucky animal days, the animals being in a 12-day cycle. This allows several possible dates for a particular festival in a lunar month, ensuring festivals in the same area do not clash and meaning that festival dates alter somewhat from year to year.

Since the end of the Cultural Revolution in 1976, festivals have grown in popularity and number, and they provide the Miao with a cultural identity.

LUSHENG FESTIVALS

This is a general name for the important courtship festivals held annually on a designated site called a 'flower ground', which could be translated as 'choosing a lover'. The lusheng festivals usually take place in January and February and are spectacular. Despite the cold weather, don't miss the opportunity to visit them. Several villages and all generations attend. Mothers bring their daughters' finery that consists of embroidered costume and silver jewellery. In only a very few areas will boys wear traditional dress; for the most part, the men have lost this custom. Festivals are usually held over a three-day period, the second and third being the most important. The girls arrive dressed in their festival costumes or don their gorgeous attire on site. A wide range of courtship rituals are practised. At Zhouxi, near Kaili, the men and boys

Drinking Rituals

The Miao, both men and women, are formidable drinkers and very hospitable people. Numerous drinking rituals vary from place to place and as all visitors to a Miao village will have to drink some of the locally-brewed spirit, it is best to learn the local customs first.

At all festivals local villagers entertain their relatives and friends with large quantities of liquor, brewed from rice, maize or potatoes. Guests are traditionally welcomed to a village with firecrackers, a musical serenade and drinks that are served as you enter. At Langde village in the Taijiang area guests are received by girls positioned at several points near the entrance to the village—at each of these points you are obliged to drink two small pottery dishes of liquor and finally, at the village gates, to drink from the horns of a water buffalo. At Miao villages near Chonganjiang red marks are stamped on your face after every two drinks using a seed head dipped in dye. These marks are to demonstrate the host's hospitality and generosity. In other areas, ash from the bottom of the wok is used to mark the guest's hands and face. Variations of this ceremony occur when entering any Miao village and it is considered very offensive is you refuse the drinks.

During any festive meal the host serves wine continually and often sings as he pours the liquor for each guest. In some areas a complicated dance ritual is performed and the lusheng pipes are played to each guest before he drinks. Many games ensure the guest drinks his share; one custom in the northwest involves sucking wine through bamboo straws. One village on the outskirts of Guiyang preserves a little wine from each bottle served to guests as a memento of the visit.

of each village play the lusheng pipes while forming a circle, the girls follow with a relatively simple dance step to show off their costumes to best advantage. The boys and men press forward to admire the girls. The girls in turn keep their eyes on the boys and, in eastern Guizhou, a girl will tie a red ribbon on her favourite's lusheng pipe. The boy returns the ribbon to the girl he is most partial to. The couple can then leave the festival ground and courtship will usually begin with the important ritual of singing to each other. In central Guizhou the young men dance while playing the lusheng pipes and, to show her attraction, a girl will tie a ribbon around a boy's waist and dance behind him, holding the other end of the ribbon. A skilful dancer may be

followed by several girls; the boy makes his choice and leads her to the edge of the circle to continue courting.

Water buffalo fighting and horse racing are exciting components of the lusheng festivals. They take place annually at several venues including the major festival at Zhouxi, near Kaili. Some villages raise bulls especially for fighting and these enjoy very special care—in summer they are protected with mosquito nets and in winter fed a special diet of green vegetables, sugar and rice wine. Before the bullfight they are scrubbed with vegetable oil and the tips of their horns are wrapped in metal. Fights usually take place on a threshing ground or out in the open. Several villages will bring their bulls to the contest. The massive animals are led in on thin ropes and are smooth and pink with shiny horns and red eyes. The drums and cymbals sound. The bulls lock horns in battle and sometimes fight to the death, but if it is obvious which bull will win the fight is stopped. Peasants leap into the fray to separate the angry bulls but sometimes a bull escapes, rushing into the crowds and scattering everyone in all directions. The winner is rewarded with red ribbons and flowers; the owner of the loser has to host a big feast to regain face. Bulls killed in the fight are often skinned, cut up, cooked and shared by everyone as part of a festival meal. Water buffalo are considered sacred and are rested one day a year on the Bull King holiday, held in their honour.

Modern events such as basketball, volleyball and table tennis competitions are increasingly a feature at the lusheng festivals. A swimming race was held at one recent riverside festival. A more traditional event is cockfighting. The local government supports these festivals and gives monetary prizes to the winners.

■ NANKAI LUSHENG FESTIVAL

The Small Flowery Miao of Nankai village, near Shuicheng in southwest Guizhou, gather for their lusheng festival on the 14th day of the second lunar month. Family groups walk at least 30 kilometres (18.6 miles) to the festival ground, washing in the nearest stream en route. They bring their own provisions, maize cobs, coal and twigs for fuel and a giant umbrella to keep off the rain. Rice and barbecued fatty pork are cooked over an open fire.

The festival lasts for three days during which the participants sleep on the hillside or stay at relatives' homes nearby. The women wear their best clothes and are often dressed in two to four layers of skirts and jackets to indicate their wealth. Their hair is piled high with huge quantities of red wool in an enormous bouffant style.

Han Chinese officials and a television crew attend the opening ceremony. When the officials leave at about 16:00, the dancing begins, led by the boys. A girl shows her liking for a boy by giving him her jacket; at the end of the evening each boy will return all jackets apart from the one given to him by his favourite. Once a couple has

Display of acrobatic lusheng pipe-playing at Nankai

formed, they court on the hillside. The girl may choose to return to the boy's home with him where they will live together for three or four months in a trial marriage. After this they will travel to the girl's village. If the trial has not proved successful as far as the boy is concerned, he will say goodbye on entering her village. She will shriek and scream and he will be chased by all the villagers—if they catch him, he will have to marry the girl. If, on the other hand, the couple are suited, marriage arrangements are made with the family. Should the girl be pregnant and unmarried, there is no feeling of disgrace and she will simply go to the next festival to find a husband. This is typical of the much freer marriage arrangements within Miao society. This freedom, however, is being altered by contact with the Han Chinese and the influence of their arranged marriage systems.

This festival also provides an opportunity for young married girls to speak to their mothers about their husbands. Girls with unhappy marriages will complain about their spouses and can be seen crying and sobbing to their mothers.

■ DANCING ON THE SLOPE FESTIVAL
The Long Horned Miao of Suoga, near Liuzhi take part in a ten-day festival between the 4th and 14th day of the first lunar month. A visit to this festival is particularly worthwhile. Local government officials arrive at the chosen flower ground on the one official day of the festival. The girls in their finery mass at the flower ground and a selection of boys play the lusheng pipes. Chosen groups of girls parade for the dignitaries who have walked two hours from the nearest road. After a couple of hours groups disperse back to their homes and more serious courting continues. Boys and girls sing to each other across the hills and the boys pursue the girls back to a chosen village where one house has been set aside as the focus of the festival. The fire is banked up and the girls crowd inside to wait for the boys to arrive. Pairs of boys outside the door sing traditional courting songs and the two named girls reply. Each pair of boys is eventually welcomed into the house and the singing continues until everyone is sitting round the fire. A communal meal is served and everybody sleeps. The following day the boys leave for the next village that has been chosen as the courting venue. Lusheng dancing takes place on the mountainside, hence the name of the festival, 'Dancing on the Slope'. Later in the evening the boys court different girls in song. Once the festival is over each boy decides which girl he wants to marry and returns to ask the girl's parents. The couple's suitability is confirmed through ritual practices after which the marriage arrangements are made.

■ SISTERS' MEAL FESTIVAL
This festival, which takes place in the spring, is easy and interesting to visit for the girls' spectacular costumes. It is probably specific to southeast Guizhou. A few days

before the festival, girls in the Shidong area flock to the mountains to collect wild flowers and berries to dye the glutinous rice known as 'sisters rice'. Each girl prepares her rice with a symbol inside and then wraps it in a handkerchief. Young people from several villages gather together, the girls beautifully dressed in their embroidered costumes. Everyone chats and the search for marriage partners commences. Towards evening the newly formed couples break away and begin singing together. The girls give their 'sisters' rice' to the boys who get an indication of the girls' true feelings from the symbols within. A pair of red chopsticks means she has accepted his hand in marriage; one chopstick, his love may not be returned; a garlic or red chilli, the boy must look elsewhere; pine needles indicate that the boy should present silks and colourful threads and that she will wait for him. The next day there are buffalo fights, horse racing, cockfights and lusheng dancing.

FERTILITY FESTIVALS

There are many local variations of the fertility festival that is enshrined in the culture of the Miao. The most important of these in southeast Guizhou is the Festival Respecting the Ancestors that takes place every 13 years. Minor festivals to respect the ancestors take place annually. During these events, the tribal chief goes to the mountains to unearth the old drum, symbolizing ancestors, that has been hidden. The two Miao ancestors, the male Zhang Yang and the female Yung Por, are represented by wooden idols with exaggerated sex organs. These are paraded through the village, Yung Por at the front and Zhang Yang at the back. A ceremony imitates copulation between the two idols, after which the drum is buried in the mountains again with a new drum. Finally, a huge feast is held for all participants, during which the most important sacrificial animal, the water buffalo, is killed. Often, in more economically stringent times, pigs are sacrificed instead.

■ GUZHANG FERTILITY FESTIVAL

The *Guzhang* ('water buffalo offal') festival takes place every 13 years, most recently in March 1992 at Langde village, Taijiang County, when modern influences mixed with age-old customs. Festivities continue for three to seven days. On the first day, the elected committee in charge of the festival climbs the mountains to search for the soul of the dragon, a symbol of good luck. The shaman guides the dragon soul into a duck, brought specifically for this purpose. In the evening, a pig is ceremonially killed and shared among all participants during a great celebratory feast. In times past, a water buffalo would have been sacrificed. Sharing the meat symbolizes sharing in the community and the preservation of old traditions that are linked with the good fortune, prosperity and fertility of the whole village. Families feast with friends and relatives from other villages late into the night.

(following pages) Long Horned Miao enjoy their lusheng festival near Liuzhi

On the second day young girls and their mothers from surrounding villages flock to Langde dressed in their best festival costumes and silver ornaments. In the centre courtyard where the festival takes place a bronze drum hangs from a green bough symbolizing life and fertility. The shaman and the organizing committee beat and circle the drum. Young girls, sumptuously attired, join the circle. As the afternoon progresses, a huge circle of dancers form, swaying slowly to the beat of the drum and the sound of the lusheng pipes. The older people join in later. Everyone drinks wine and peasants from the surrounding area hang coloured ribbons on the bough where the drum is hanging. The music and dancing continues for four to six hours until the girls gradually drop out.

Feasting and more drinking then begins in the village. The shaman chants, lights incense and burns paper money before the organizing committee prepares its own meal and sits to eat and discuss the festival. This committee, which has raised the necessary funds for the festival, extends hospitality to anyone passing by. Meanwhile the young are once again gathering in the courtyard. The Youth Federation of the village has invited an entertainment troupe from another village to perform. This troupe dances and sings to the tunes of the 1990s with the most up-to-date routines while the young people look on. Only a few of the performing troupe play traditional melodies. The Youth Federation, identified by a red armband, ensure everyone is well-behaved and that order is maintained.

On the third day, the drum beats in the early afternoon signifying the start of another dance ceremony, this time attended by even more people. The shaman ends the dancing in the evening with offerings and an official photograph is taken.

Dragon Festivals
■ DRAGON BOAT FESTIVAL

Held on the Qingshui River between the 24th and 27th of the fifth lunar month, this festival is well worth seeing. The Miao come from Taijiang, Zhenyuan and Shibing to take part. The origin of this festival is explained by the folk story of a dragon that swallowed a fisherman's son. Guya, the fisherman, retaliated and burnt the dragon's home. The fire burned for nine days and finally the people celebrated the fisherman's victory by eating the dragon meat. Five villages in the area received different parts of the dragon's anatomy—each of these villages now holds a dragon festival on a different day to celebrate his destruction. A 17-metre (56-foot) boat and two 10-metre (33-foot) boats are constructed from fir, each with a carved dragon's head on its prow. The boats are launched and over 40 rowers drink fiery spirits. They row to the villages where pleas are made to the dragon to bestow happiness on each community. Pigs, goats, ducks and geese are presented to the crew and headman. Families gather on the bank to eat and gossip and in the evenings the young people sing to each other.

A Diluvial Tale

In the legend of the flood, two persons survived, a brother and a sister, who were saved in a huge bottle-gourd. The brother wished the sister to be his wife, but she objected to this as not being proper. At length she suggested to her brother that one should take the upper and the other the nether millstone and going to the tops of opposite hills roll the stones down into the valley between. If these stones should be found in the valley one upon the other after the manner of millstones, she would consent to be his wife, but not if the stones were found lying apart. The brother agreed to this proposal; but considering how unlikely it was that two stones rolled down from opposite hills should meet and be found in the position required, he surreptitiously placed two millstones one on top of the other in the valley. Then from the hill-tops they rolled down the stones, which were lost on the hillsides; and on reaching the valley he showed the sister the stones as he had placed them. She, however, was not satisfied, and proposed that a box should be placed in the valley, and that each from opposite hills should throw a knife into the valley. If both the knives were found in the box they should marry, but not otherwise. Again the brother, thinking how unlikely it was that both the knives should find the box, put two knives in it before starting up the hill. Both the knives thrown from the hill-tops were lost, but when the sister saw the two knives her brother had placed in the box, she consented to be his wife. In course of time a child was born, deaf, dumb, and without arms and legs. The father was so enraged that he killed the child, cut it in pieces, and threw them about on the hillside. Next morning these pieces had changed into men and women, and in this way the earth was repeopled.

William Edgar Geil, Eighteen Capitals of China, 1911

While travelling in Guizhou, William Geil heard this story of the origins of the Miao, which he has reproduced from records of the West China Missionary Conference.

Miao Menus

The different groups of Miao specialize in their own culinary delicacies but all Miao are hospitable and will press food on a guest with tremendous enthusiasm and generosity. Even during times of scarcity, the Miao believe it is only right and natural that a guest should be honoured with food. A guest's rice bowl will be constantly filled and he or she will be given the best titbits. Guests, in turn, should always show appreciation for the food and enjoy everything offered, but remember it is considered polite to leave some food in your bowl. Pork fat is a staple and a favourite when friends visit, often served as you enter the household with the customary welcoming drinks. The Miao travel with cured fat to festivals; this is barbecued over a fire and eaten with rice as a main meal. The meals below give some idea of the cuisine of southeast Guizhou.

Everyday meal eaten with a Miao family in the Huaxi area:
    Tofu (bean curd) deep fried in pig fat
    Peas with small pieces of chopped pork and chilli
    Sliced kohlrabi with chilli
    Potatoes and sweet potatoes cooked in the fire in their skins
    Sour fish soup made of pickled tomatoes, fish, bean sprouts, wild chives
        and stock
    Rice

Festival meal eaten with the Miao of Taijiang:
    Rice and maize wine served liberally
    Diced cooked beef (water buffalo preferred) with celery and chilli
    Chopped pork cooked with mushrooms and chilli
    Cold root salad seasoned with ground chilli pepper
    Wood-ear fungi, garlic, chopped pork and chilli
    Hundred-year-old egg
    Fish chopped and stir-fried
    Barbecued pork cut in slices
    Chicken and vegetable soup
    Stir-fried fresh green mustard
    Sausages made of blood, bean curd, pork fat; dried and wood-smoked
    Peanuts
    Well-seasoned omelette
    Rice

(above) *Glutinous rice cakes stamped with good luck symbols;* (below) *Miao meal in Taijiang*

■ TAIJIANG DRAGON LANTERN FESTIVAL

This festival is celebrated with great gusto in Taijiang, near Kaili, where the entertainment takes on a unique flavour. Several groups in Taijiang from the period of the 1st to the 15th of the first lunar month make large paper dragons that are manipulated by 10–15 men. Children are given straw dragons. On the 15th night they weave through the streets stopping at different households. Each householder gives them money and liquor to ensure good luck for the family in the year to come. However, if there has been a death in the family during the preceding year, the dragon cannot enter. The main street is filled with people three to four deep to watch the dragons. Part of the fun is to destroy them with giant homemade fireworks made from bamboo and packed with gunpowder. These are lit and the flames directed at the dragons. The centre of activity is outside the local government building where all the dragons come to receive money. Often there are as many as 30 to 50 dragons to destroy. The excitement continues until midnight with the unmarried ending the occasion by singing love songs to each other.

Marriage

Festivals are the most important of the ways for boys and girls to meet each other. Miao society offers a greater degree of freedom than many others with the one taboo against intermarriage within the same clan. The preferred spouse for a son is the mother's brother's daughter. Occasionally a girl will be promised in marriage at birth if two families wish to stengthen ties, but in general the girls have a certain amount of individual choice.

In the Taijiang area the custom of 'stealing a wife' was common, though less so nowadays. This involves a young couple eloping for several days. On their return, the boy asks his family to invite the girl's family to a banquet. The most eloquent male of the household is chosen to visit the girl's parents to plead for her hand in marriage on the boy's behalf. The spokesman will take a chicken with him—if an agreement is reached, the chicken will be ceremonially killed, if not, the chicken will be thrown out of the house. This, however, rarely happens as it would mean the couple leaving the area to elope permanently without the support of either family. Formal wedding arrangements are made soon after both families give their consent.

Festivals, often the beginning of a romance, allow the boy's parents to assess the wealth of the girl's family by the silver ornaments she wears. Much admired traditional skills such as the embroidery on a girl's costume can also be judged. Nowadays, however, Miao families recognize that embroidery can be bought and may not be worked by the girl herself, so other factors are considered. These include her ability for hard work, her looks and, particularly among those living near towns and open to modern influences, her educational achievements. Urban-minded boys admire modern clothing and will be interested in how a girl dresses in her daily life. The two families involved will investigate each other before agreeing to a marriage; if either side is plagued by an evil spirit or bad ghost, it will be called off. The traditional criteria for choosing a wife are changing however—arranged marriages are increasing as wealth becomes a more significant factor for both families. A bride price has to be agreed. In the past, this payment by the boy's family was made in silver, now modern commodities such as a bicycle or television are common and in some areas, cash that can vary from from 1,000 to 1,800 *yuan*. If the groom cannot pay for his bride, he may work for her family to cover the bride price. The girl's family is responsible for quilts, some furniture and for her jewellery.

Marriage ceremonies differ between areas but it is common for the bride to be collected by unmarried male friends of the groom. She is dressed in a beautiful embroidered costume with all the silver she possesses and is taken to the groom's house. Her silver represents her wealth and remains with her all her life. Her family will also give her a small present, such as chickens, so she retains some independence and is able to buy items like embroidery silks for herself from selling chicks or eggs. The wedding will be accompanied by much feasting and drinking and in some areas a bamboo cane is broken to symbolize the union. The girl remains with her new husband for several nights, but in some regions will return to her family on the day of the wedding. She will spend time with her husband during festival occasions and traditionally did not return to his house until becoming pregnant. As there is considerable sexual freedom in Miao society she may have had sex with another man in the meantime, which is why in some cases the first child does not inherit the family land. Today, the bride usually returns to her husband's house after two weeks bearing more gifts and again dressed in her finest clothes.

In areas where the different ethnic groups live side by side, intermarriage has occurred and superficially there do not appear to be any current taboos. Close to or within the urban areas, ethnic people and Han Chinese intermarry. Prior to 1949, this would have been considered a poor marriage by the Han who looked down on the Miao. Some prejudice may remain today.

Suggested Tour Itineraries

There are several excellent itineraries for visiting the various groups of Miao, depending on the length of time you have and on the level of comfort—or adventure—you are prepared to accept.

(clockwise from top left) *Welcoming guests with buffalo horns of wine, Langde;
Miao lusheng dance performance for tourists; welcoming guests with sweet potatoes and tea,
near Kaili; Black Miao women pose in traditional costume*

Miao men play flutes (left) while women sing (right) at Huaxi, near Guiyang

■ ITINERARY ONE

For those wanting de luxe hotels, stay at **Guiyang** and **Anshun** and visit the Miao in these localities. You can arrange with GZOTC and CITS to see traditional dance and musical performances and enjoy meals with the villagers.

■ ITINERARY TWO

More adventurous travellers can go from Guiyang to **Kaili** to spend several days visiting different groups of Miao in the area before travelling on to **Taijiang**, staying overnight at the Chinese-style hotel and then on to **Shidong** where there are only basic facilities. Driving on to **Tongren**, where there is a reasonable hotel, stay one night before travelling to Zhangjiajie National Forest Park in Hunan Province for its spectacular limestone scenery and Miao people. You can round off this ten-day itinerary by travelling to **Changsha**, the capital of Hunan Province.

■ ITINERARY THREE

A ten-day itinerary in western Guizhou allows you to see quite different groups of Miao. Travel from Guiyang to **Anshun** and stay two nights visiting Miao in the area. You can meet other Miao groups if you travel on and stay one or two nights at each of the centres of **Liuzhi**, **Shuicheng** and **Weining**. You can then take a train or travel by road from Shuicheng to **Kunming** in Yunnan Province. The hotels vary from reasonable to basic.

■ ITINERARY FOUR

You can visit interesting Black Miao groups in southwest Guizhou (see page 194).

Song of Creation

*If the Miao have no literature, they have plenty of legends handed down
from earlier times. Who composed these legends no one knows; they are
taught by the older people to the girls and boys. Many of them are in verse,
five syllables to a line, the stanzas being of unequal length, one stanza
interrogative and one responsive. These are sung or recited at their festivals
by two persons or two groups, generally one group of young men and one
group of young women, one group interrogating and the other responding.
Among these legends, which I have written down from the dictation of my
Heh Miao teacher, is a story of the Creation and a story of the Flood. The
story of Creation commences:*

> Who made heaven and earth?
> Who made insects?
> Who made men?
> Made male and made female?
>   I who speak don't know.

> Vang-vai (Heavenly King) made heaven and earth.
> Zie-ne made insects.
> Zie-ne made men and demons,
> Made male and made female.
>   How is it you don't know?

> How made heaven and earth?
> How made insects?
> How made men and demons?
> Made male and made female?
>   I who speak don't know.

> Heavenly King is (or was) intelligent.
> Spat a lot of spittle into his hand,
> Clapped his hands with a noise,

Produced heaven and earth.
Tall wild grass made insects.
Stones made men and demons.
Made male and made female.
　　　　How is it you don't know?

Made heaven in what way?
Made earth in what way?
　　　　Thus by rote I sing,
　　　　But don't understand.

Made heaven like a sun-hat.
Made earth like a dust-pan.
　　　　Why don't you understand?
Made heaven a single lump,
Made earth a single lump.

Who put heaven up?
Heaven then so very high.
Who separated earth low down?
Earth then deep and low.
　　　　I sing and don't understand.

The poem then goes on to relate how heaven and earth were kept apart after they were separated. They tried all sorts of wood and all sorts of metal, and at length decided to prop up heaven with pillars made of silver. But where were they to get fire to melt the silver? Fire had gone up to heaven; how were they to bring it down? Fire eventually came down from heaven in a stone, and with raw steel and tinder they extracted the fire from the stone. After heaven had been propped up with silver pillars, the sun and moon and milky-way were fixed in their places. The sun, however, went away and would not come back. Thereupon they sent various beasts and birds to call the sun to return, but they would not go; or if they went, the sun refused to come at their call. Finally, they sent the cock to call the sun to return, and when the cock crew the sun came back. The poem concludes that the proof of this is that when the cock crows the sun rises!

Samuel R Clarke, Among the Tribes in South-west China, *1911*

Textiles, Costumes and Silver of the Miao

Clothing identifies the society to which a person belongs as well as giving an individual identity within the society. Miao women and girls from different areas wear very specific costumes, hairstyles and silver ornaments. This strong identification through dress may have arisen because of the Miao's frequent migrations in the past. Clothing differs somewhat for married and unmarried women. Festival dress indicates wealth and skill in a number of crafts such as weaving, embroidery and batik. These skills are judged important in the selection of a marriage partner, indicating a girl's diligence and domesticity.

Before marriage, girls either embroider or make a batik baby carrier, depending on the particular group. Some of the finest work is reserved for these baby carriers as a girl's skill, and hence her position in society, will be judged by this most important item of traditional costume. Before and after marriage she makes baby clothes with many symbols to ward off evil spirits and to ensure long life and good fortune for the child—mortality rates are high in the agricultural society and infants need to be protected. Baby hats are exquisitely embroidered with good luck symbols and often with the faces of lions or tigers to scare off evil spirits. Children are esteemed as they continue the family line, are a source of labour and look after their parents in old age.

Straw rain cape

Costumes have retained their importance in Miao society, especially among women. The men in the countryside more commonly wear the rural dress of Han peasants, blue or black jackets and trousers. Only a few Miao groups had a tradition of special male festival costume. Today most older men wear Mao jackets (*sun zhong shan*) and trousers while the younger men wear Western-style trousers, shirts and sweaters.

Guizhou is a particularly wet province and the peasants work outdoors in all weathers. Traditionally, capes of straw or palm leaves kept off the rain; these have largely given way to plastic although you will still see straw capes. A cape of date palm fibres protects clothing from baskets carried on the back. Many Miao women living near the towns and cities wear modern clothes but in the countryside most continue to wear traditional costume, notably the middle-aged and elderly. For festival events, the vast majority of Miao women, old and young, wear traditional dress that varies with the region.

Big Flowery Miao woman weaving, near Weining

Embroidery designs, materials and techniques in the east of the province have been subject to greater influence by those of the Han Chinese because of the good transport links to the middle Chang Jiang (Yangzi) basin via the Qingshui River and tributaries. Here you will find some of the most elaborate, rich and beautifully designed costumes. Silver adornment in this area is more widespread. The northwest, with its poor natural resources and difficult communication links, produces high-quality workmanship and interesting techniques but costumes are not as rich as in the east and southeast. Festival costumes here are decorated with woven pieces, appliqué and batik; designs are geometric and jewellery is relatively scarce. Central and southern Guizhou have a rich tradition of embroidery and because these areas have been influenced by styles from the east and northwest, there is a tremendous range of decorative techniques.

The introduction of tourism to Guizhou in 1987 has affected the Miao, particularly in the more accessible southeast. Villages near main roads and those within reach of a minibus journey have been opened to tourists. Villagers give song and dance performances and then sell their textiles to the visitiors. Tourism has thus encouraged local culture and in some cases has revived ethnicity and intensified ritualism. Textiles are being produced to supply tourists and traders who sell them in hotels throughout southwest China. To get a better price, Miao women travel long distances to sell their textiles outside hotels in the towns of Guizhou. In some cases, as has been observed in Kaili, this has led to costumes of different groups being mixed—the women may be selling costumes of which they have no knowledge. Wrongly-labelled, mismatching costumes are often sold in Han Chinese shops in other provinces. Tourists have undoubtedly provided a new source of income for the women and encouraged the production of textiles. With the surplus money earned, women spend more on their daughters' festival and wedding costumes. Tourism has thus helped to keep alive traditional textile skills. However, the downside of modernization in the countryside of Guizhou could be the gradual disappearance of the rich variety of costumes as traditional values and ways of life are discarded.

GZOTC and CITS both arrange textile tours, or more adventurous travellers can visit the villages directly, to see various techniques including spinning, weaving, dyeing, embroidery, batik and other unique and intricate textile arts.

Fibres

Most country women spin and weave their own cloth, supplemented by some commercial fabrics. Hemp and other similar plants indigenous to China were the main fibres used by both the Han Chinese and the ethnic groups. Silk was the preserve of the wealthy and those at court. Cotton was introduced to southwest China during the Han period (206 BC–AD 220) from India, but hemp predominated among the rural classes throughout China. Cotton was not used extensively until the middle of the 20th century when cheap cotton cloth was mass-produced. Ramie, a finer cloth than hemp, is now being produced from a plant belonging to the nettle family.

■ HEMP

Although hemp production is decreasing because land is needed for cash crops and manufactured cotton is readily available, it is still grown, spun and woven in remote mountain villages in Guizhou. The mountain people use hemp by choice as it is much stronger and wears better than cotton.

Hemp fibres are made from the leaves and stalks that are cut several times during the summer. In some areas the leaves are stripped off and discarded while the stalks, which are approximately 2 metres (6.6 feet) in height, are tied into bundles and carried back to the village. These are dried in the sun or around a fire. When the sap has dried out the women pull out the fibres with their fingernails and twist them in their fingers to form a thread. This is skeined and then bleached by boiling for several hours in water and ash. The fibres are softened by pounding and spun onto bobbins. Beeswax can be added to make it smooth and pliant, after which it is pounded again to thicken the thread before weaving. Hemp cloth is much coarser than cotton but it wears well and softens with washing.

■ COTTON

Some villages in east Guizhou grow cotton but the quality is poor and, because of the rain, the colour tends to yellow. It is grown and spun by the Miao of the south. Raw cotton for weaving from other areas of China supplements local supplies, but the abundance of cheap manufactured cotton material has led to a decline in this sort of weaving.

■ SILK

Silk is produced only on a limited scale today. A number of villages in southeast Guizhou used to breed silkworms. Sericulture is said to have come with the Miao when they migrated from the middle reaches of the Chang Jiang (Yangzi River). As elsewhere in China, the larvae are fed on mulberry leaves. However, unlike that in the Chang Jiang basin or Xi Jiang (Pearl River) delta, the Miao do not prune the tree annually nor grow it on a large scale along the paddy fields. In Guizhou, mulberry trees grow near villages or wild on the hillsides up to an altitude of 1,800 metres (5,905 feet). The scale of production must have been small in former times—no mulberry trees are shown in any of the distribution maps in the 1937 book, *Land Utilisation in China*. It is safe to assume the Miao produced silk only for domestic use including embroidery silks and to make ornate strips for decorating costumes and baby carriers, examples of which continue in the Taijiang area.

In villages near Kaili, fine patterned silk is woven and is a major decoration for baby carriers. Locals confirmed that in the past, most households would rear silkworms through the whole life cycle, but few do so today. Pedlars now bring eggs, produced in a specialized unit outside Anshun, a distance of at least 200 kilometres (124 miles) to sell to villagers. The woman of the household places the eggs on a basket, stores them carefully in a barn and when hatched feeds the larvae daily with mulberry leaves. Once the larvae have spun a silk cocoon the pupae are killed by plunging them into boiling water after which the women unreel the silk. A few families living in remote areas in the southeast keep the pupae to develop into butterflies, producing eggs for the following year. You might find silkworms on sale at markets around Taijiang in May. This relieves the women of the complicated task of keeping the eggs warm over the cold winter months, a very time-consuming job on a small scale. Raw natural silk, synthetic threads and dyed embroidery silks are also available at the markets. Commercial production of silk is being considered in several areas of southwest China and in Liupanshui.

■ SILK FELT

This exceptionally interesting and unique fabric is made in southeast Guizhou on a very limited scale. Silkworms, when ready to spin their cocoons, are placed on a flat wooden board. They cannot find anywhere to rest and so move backwards and forwards leaving a trail of threads which tangle together. This is then matted by rolling

In Search of the Indigo Secret

Vegetable dyes giving an indigo blue colour have been used extensively in China for centuries but little work has been done on the plants that produce the dye substance, *indigotin*. Indigo (*landian* in Chinese) is completely different from other vegetable dyes and can be obtained from a number of plants in different genuses. It is commonly thought *polygonum* is used in China and the ethnic groups in southwest China may use the *indigofera tinctoria* that is used by the Hmong in Thailand. During research by the author in Guizhou from 1990 to 1993, a number of plants used by the ethnic groups were identified. In the southeast, southwest and the Dong area, *strobilanthes cusia* (formerly *flaccidifolius*), an evergreen shrub propagated by basal cuttings, was found growing and was being soaked in wooden barrels to produce a dye paste. Fresh cuttings of *strobilanthes* are planted at the beginning of the year to yield rich green leaves that are picked from July to make the indigo paste. *Indigofera* was found only occasionally in the southeast, *polygonum tinctoria* was found in the southeast but not the southwest. These plants are difficult to locate—peasants tuck them into small fields between vegetables, rice and other cash crops. Indigo root cuttings are sometimes sold by the Miao at the local markets. Other genuses are seeded.

A dye vat is started from a paste, made from the plants immediately on harvesting, so that indigo dyeing can continue year-round. The paste is made in slightly different ways but a sequence emerged. Leaves of the indigo plant are cut between July and October and carried down from the peasant's plot in baskets on shoulder poles to handmade wooden barrels, usually near a river or water source. Several baskets of leaves are put in the barrel, wedged down by various basketry devices and then covered with water. The barrels are left to stand and the fermentation process begins. This job, usually performed by women, can take between three days and several weeks, depending on the temperature. When the fermentation process is judged complete, the leaves are removed, lime is added and the contents of

Strobilanthes cusia, near Taijiang

the barrel are beaten to introduce oxygen so that it froths. The mixture is left to stand for a time; a crusty blue froth is usually a good indicator that this step is over. The water is then drained off with scoops, often made from gourds. The indigo paste left at the bottom is poured off into baskets. Many groups among the Miao, Dong, Bouyei and Shui keep a wooden vat in their household to dye their own woven pieces. The vat is kept going all year and is fed with the dye paste that is stored in baskets.

In some villages women send their cloth to be dyed by a specialist. One Bouyei village near Zhenfeng, southwest Guizhou, does not grow indigo to make paste, but buys it on market days from an area nearby. The master dyer of this village, a man, explained that he had kept his dye vat going for ten years, feeding it every night with different quantities of paste and lime, according to the desired colour of the fabric he was dyeing, and a very small proportion of industrial soda. The following day he would inspect his vat and test the indigo with his hand to see if it would produce the right shade of blue. If the feel is not quite right he adds a little rice wine. Several dippings of the cloth give rise to darker shades of blue. In Dong villages it is the women who make the paste and do the dyeing.

In areas of southeast and southwest Guizhou, some peasants only make indigo paste for sale in the markets. Interestingly, the Han Chinese have also become involved in this trade and have set up a specialized indigo production area near Kaili. Villages near main roads often use chemical rather than natural indigo and itinerant dyers will dye yarn or cloth at weekly markets.

Miao woman selling indigo paste

so the fibres cling together forming silk felt. The number of silkworms determines the thickness of the felt. The felt is dyed and cut into shapes that are used as colourful motifs by Miao women outside Kaili on their festive dress. University professors at Guiyang believe this method was used in the past by the Bouyei to produce a fine cloth for their dead and by the Shui for their baby carriers and costumes. A second method of making silk felt involves the coarse outer silk floss from the cocoon being layered on a board, pounded and then rolled. The exact extent of this practice is not known.

Dyes

Vegetable dyes are still used on a limited scale in remote areas but chemical dyes are readily available in the markets and are used extensively. Guizhou Province stands out as one of the increasingly few areas of the world where natural indigo and the processes involved in dyeing with it can still be seen. Natural indigo paste and indigo root cuttings are sold at markets. However, even with indigo that is the most popular of dyes, chemical replacements are creeping in.

Dyers using purely chemical dyes of all colours set up at markets, and even professional indigo dyers, for example near Duyun, are using chemical indigo additives to achieve a darker blue colour more quickly. The young are not so interested in the traditional methods of indigo dyeing as it is a messy and time-consuming process; the dyer's hands are permanently stained blue and dye vats require constant attention and care.

In 1992, the provincial and local governments decided that indigo should be kept a secret—it was feared particularly that dyeing techniques would be copied by the Japanese who have a specific interest in traditional textiles. Foreigners are therefore not generally allowed to see indigo or discuss it with local people. General interest in indigo is accepted but formal study is prohibited.

Indigo paste is now being produced on a commercial basis near Zhenfeng and in a number of other small areas in southeast Guizhou. The Han Chinese have set up large indigo gardens that are usually harvested in June and October. The leaves are processed in large vats producing a concentrated indigo paste that is sold to the Miao throughout the year in the markets. This is typical of the small enterprises that developed during the 1980s. Synthetic indigo is also used and pedlars bring vats to the markets so the women can dye their cloth on the spot.

After dyeing and drying, some Miao calender their cloth by beating it with a wooden mallet or with stone to make it shiny and lustrous. Egg white is painted onto cloth to give a glossy sheen in some areas such as Rongjiang in the southeast. Pig's

Dong woman soaks leaves to make indigo paste

blood or the liquid from boiled beef sinews is sometimes applied with a brush to give a brownish-red tone. In Taijiang a cowhide is boiled and the glue applied to the dyed cloth, probably to fix the indigo.

Weaving

In the low agricultural season you will hear the clatter of looms being worked in many Miao villages. A wide range of looms is used and the techniques are generally highly sophisticated. There are many expert weavers who produce intricate designs. Young girls in most villages are taught to weave from an early age as it is still considered important for them to weave their own festival and wedding clothes. Weavers concentrate their skills on traditional pieces for turbans and aprons, others create a twill-weave cloth and the honeycomb weave that is used to make jackets in the Taijiang area. Another Miao group living near Kaili produces a range of tartan fabrics, worn by the children, that often have a cotton warp and silk weft. Hemp is woven in more remote areas, wool in northeast Guizhou.

■ BRAIDING
Cotton and silk braid in many intricate designs is produced on several types of loom by Miao women all over Guizhou. The Gejia use a backstrap loom, holding the warp on their big toe. Young girls learn to weave braid from the age of seven and progress from this to more complex pieces.

Embroidery

The craft of embroidery is part of the Chinese heritage. In times past, while living alongside the Han Chinese, the Miao would have had contact with their skills, techniques and designs. Today the Miao have a rich and unique tradition of embroidery although little is really known about its history. This richness cannot be explained except by the fact that they had no written tradition; it is postulated that the embroideries replace the written word and tell the story of Miao evolution, their flight from north China and their myths.

As in central China, embroidery among the Miao was probably the preserve of wealthy peasants and landlords. A peasant woman today mentioned that before Liberation, her family could not afford embroidered clothes. The Guizhou Miao of the early 20th century have been described as living in hovels, too poor for clothing and ekeing out a living from the poorest area of China. Salisbury, in *The Long March*,

Miao hand-woven apron with central stylized dragon

Embroidered sleeve panels (clockwise from top left): *two dragons with pearl of wisdom protecting mother butterfly figure; figurative heroine riding a bird; double dragon; geometric stylized dragons;*

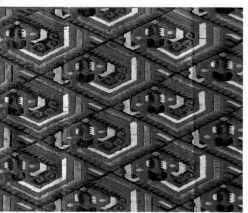 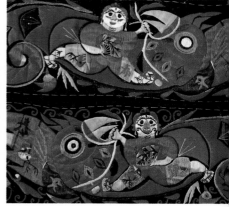

notes that children had to share clothes. Certainly there was no mention of the rich costume or gorgeous silk embroidery that abounds today.

Jackets are embellished with embroidery in a wide range of designs and needle-work techniques. Embroidery is also skilfully worked into aprons, baby carriers and, to a lesser degree, skirts. Some of the best embroidery is found on the baby carriers. In the southeast, skirts are sometimes embroidered round the hem with three lines, said to represent the main rivers crossed by the Miao on their journey to Guizhou; the Huang He (Yellow River), the Hui and the Chang Jiang (Yangzi River).

As well as the coloured silk threads used to such stunning effect in their work, the Miao often incorporate gold paper cutouts and metal sequins into their embroidery designs.

Batik

China has a long history of batik production dating back to the sixth century but the batik of southwest China developed independently. In Guizhou, batik work embellishes women's costume and is used on both skirts and jackets.

The Miao and the Bouyei use a dye-resist method that is different from the Han Chinese batik process. Miao legend tells how a poor girl was staying at home to weave because she had no clothes to wear to the festival. A beehive on the ceiling dropped to the ground, splashing the cloth with wax. Despite this mishap, she dyed her cloth and then removed the wax. She found a design under the wax and from then on, she experimented by applying wax in patterns. She was thus able to go to the lusheng festival the following year with a beautiful new costume.

Before the cloth is batiked it is stretched on a board and, in the case of hemp, softened by rubbing with a stone. Batik is made by drawing molten beeswax directly onto the fabric. Beeswax is collected in April and May and kept for several months to give a darker colour that is easier to work with. A variety of pen-like instruments are used to draw the design. After heating, the wax is kept liquid by storing it in a container insulated with husks of rice. The fabric is dyed, usually in indigo, the wax acting as a dye-resist, then boiled to remove the wax, rinsed in cool water and air-dried. The beeswax can be reused.

The Gejia are highly skilled in this craft and they use batik pre-eminently to decorate their costumes. They use very finely drawn circular and spiral designs representing the horns of the water buffalo, symbolizing their ancestors' life and death. Girls start learning to produce batik from the age of six or seven years. The finest work is found on baby carriers, sleeves of their jackets and skirts. Wax resist dyeing is a very slow process; it takes a Gejia girl between one and five years to complete a single set of clothes for her marriage, working in her leisure time. Girls are usually helped by their mothers to produce the other two sets required before marriage.

Many Miao groups throughout the province also produce batik and as the designs are very individual, they can be used to identify specific villages or areas. In the northwest, for example, the work is less skilled, with larger, more open designs. However, the work of all regions is of great interest for studying traditional designs.

Women's Costume

A rich diversity of costume exists among the Miao of Guizhou. A typical Miao woman's festival costume consists of an exquisitely embroidered cotton or silk jacket or cape. Embroidered pieces replete with symbolic meaning are attached to the sleeves,

Batik scroll by Hu Jun, inspired by Miao technique and contact with Western art

jacket edges and sometimes the back of the jacket. Occasionally the embroidery is worked directly onto the jacket or skirt. Skirts of varying lengths are usually made of pleated cotton or hemp. Despite the strong tradition of Miao costume, the influence of the prevailing Chinese culture has made its mark—as early as the

Gejia girl skilfully applys beeswax on cotton to produce batik

1920s some girls, especially from the Taijiang area, were wearing the more comfortable fitted jackets and trousers in the Han style.

Festival costumes are skilfully worked and highly valued by the girls because each set can take months or even years to weave and embroider. Should it rain, a festival is immediately cancelled, or if in progress, will be abandoned because the girls do not want to risk spoiling their costumes—dyes are not generally colourfast and the pleats in their skirts could fall out.

■ SKIRTS

A most important characteristic of the costume of the Miao is the pleated skirt, worn by most but not all groups. The length of the skirt depends on the group. In the southeast a cotton skirt is traditionally prepared by weaving strips about 45 centimetres (18 inches) wide and joining them together. If a skirt has no seams, the cloth has been manufactured commercially. Pleats can be achieved in a variety of ways.

Miao in the Chonganjiang area explained that they pleat their skirts by sewing several rows of running stitch 30 centimetres (12 inches) apart, starching the skirt heavily and then drawing it up and drying it slowly away from the sun. In the Taijiang area, the skirt length is placed loosely around a barrel and tied on by a cord. Pleats are pulled into place with a sharp pointed instrument and sprinkled constantly with starch. The barrel and the cloth are then left to dry in the sun. The stiffener is made by boiling cowhide. Bamboo lengths are tied together into a cylinder and this is used to dry the skirt on. In the Kaili and Taijiang areas skirts are reputed to have over five hundred pleats and to have been inspired originally by the gills of a mushroom. The book, *Clothings and Ornaments of China's Miao People*, describes the process of making a skirt in the Rongshui area of northeast Guangxi, bordering Guizhou:

A finely batiked and embroidered skirt
worn by the Long Horned Miao, near Liuzhi

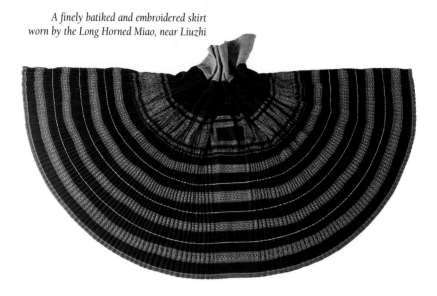

In Rongshui area the usual length of a pleated skirt is 50 cm (20 inches) and the width over 6 m (20 feet). It is pieced together with eighteen pieces of homemade cloth of narrow width. It takes three skilled women three days to make a pleated skirt by the continuous process. The process begins with placing a piece of shiny cloth on a wooden board, firstly starching and beating it, then drawing vertical lines evenly on both sides. Afterwards the cloth is folded along the lines and both ends are sewn up tightly. The folded piece is tied up on a semicircular piece of bamboo, put into a thick bamboo tube and steamed for an hour. Then the folded cloth is taken out and air-dried. Thus the pleats of the skirt are given a permanent set and will not deform in course of time.

■ JACKETS

Jackets come in many forms and are decorated in different ways, each specific to the group, village or area. In the southeast, jackets are heavily and intricately embroidered. The material of the jacket is very stiff and, as they often embroider outdoors, the girls prefer to work on small pieces that they can carry with them and only later stitch onto the jackets. These pieces can also be used to replace damaged pieces or, if the body of the jacket wears out, they can be taken off and reused. Some damaged embroidery pieces and those belonging to the older women are often overdyed by brushing on indigo, giving a dark colour. By contrast, jackets in the northwest among the Big Flowery Miao tend to be more like capes that are decorated with woven pieces and appliqué work. The Little Flowery Miao also wear a cape-like jacket with exquisite cross-stitch in geometric designs.

Within the southeast, designs and techniques used in the sleeve pieces differ enormously. Near Taijiang, at Shidong, sleeve pieces are decorated in a highly pictorial style with birds, flowers, animals and insects found in the creation story as well as with Miao heroes. The patterns for these sleeve designs are obtained in several ways. A particularly artistic girl will design her own in the style of her area but it is more common for girls to buy papercuts. Women of the older generation who retain the traditional knowledge draw a pattern on a sheet of paper under which are seven other sheets held together with cotton paper plugs. The pattern is then cut out and the designs are sold. The embroiderer will keep the top copy as a master sheet from which to work; the other copies are tacked onto the base fabric and embroidered over. Outline patterns are also available at the markets that are pounced onto the material to be embroidered. In other villages in the region, the embroidery tends to be strongly geometric, expressing the Miao love of colour and design rather than reflecting historical or mythological events.

A pleated Gejia batik and embroidery skirt with hand-woven straps

Some groups are particularly skilled at appliqué. Outside Kaili, the Miao decorate their jackets with complex mitred patchwork, known in the UK in the 1970s as Somerset patchwork. Folded silk is arranged into exquisite geometric designs. Pictorial designs of birds, fish and Miao dragons with the head of a water buffalo and tail of a silkworm are also incorporated into this appliqué patchwork.

Pieces are often outlined with braid work. This is laborious and dexterous work. A number of silk threads are passed over each other in a pattern on a small frame. The braid is then couched onto the material of the sleeve piece. More expensive embroidered pieces are decorated with braid that is pleated and then couched to give a relief effect.

■ APRONS

The aprons of the Taijiang and Kaili area tend to be highly pictorial, often depicting the creation story and other Miao legends. You will also see many of the Han Chinese auspicious symbols, for example the bat, signifying happiness, or the Taoist gourd alongside more contemporary themes and designs—Tiananmen Square, Chinese

Miao woman's jacket from Zhouxi, used for her wedding day, c. 1930

Embroidered Miao sleeve panel, Taijiang

Exquisitely embroidered back of a Miao jacket, Huangping

A shaman's jacket, known as a Hundred Bird coat, from southeast Guizhou

characters and copies of the mass-produced factory designs of the 1960s such as goldfish and peonies. Girls also embroider what they see in their immediate environment. Designs evolve relatively slowly and there is not much striking originality; conforming to traditional design is considered more important. The Miao of the southeast also produce sophisticated woven aprons, often using a supplementary weft technique, in geometric or stylized pictorial designs. The ties for the aprons are worked in many fine coloured silks and provide further outstanding evidence of the Miao weaving skills and of the care they take with every detail.

■ SHOES
The old tradition of embroidered shoes has practically disappeared although you might see some examples at the festivals. Embroidered insoles are still popular and are worked particularly by the older women.

Hairstyles

Hairstyles vary greatly and are an integral part of the Miao woman's costume, often denoting marital status. The men in Guizhou have Western-style haircuts but the women, including those who do not wear traditional costume, nearly always keep their hair long and in the traditional style. Girls begin to arrange their hair at the age of six or seven and by the time they are 14–16 years old they pay great attention to the style that is totally individual for each group. Hair is swept into buns and knots of varying size or arranged in huge structures supported with extra hair or wooden pieces. Oil holds the hair in place and gives it a shine. Some groups use a turban as an integral part of the style that is wrapped round the head in a specific way. Hair is also decorated with wooden combs, now often replaced with plastic combs and flowers. Silver combs are used at festivals. The most exotic hairstyle is at Puding and Liuzhi where vast quantities of false hair is wound around two wooden horns over which the girl's own hair is carefully brushed. The false hair is from a female ancestor, usually a mother, and a girl will also collect her own hair throughout her life. This enormous bouffant style, over 80 centimetres (31 inches) across and weighing as much as 3 kilograms (6.6 pounds), is worn by the young girls at festivals. The weight is such that a girl's real hair often wears away. In the Shuicheng area, the girls use red wool and brush their own hair over the top of this. In sharp contrast, married women of the Tall-Pointed Hat Miao shave off their hair to accommodate their hat. A common practice among many Miao women is to pluck the hair from above the forehead to give them a high brow, enhancing their beauty.

Silver

Silver, symbol of beauty, wealth and nobility, is the most revered of Miao adornments. Silver is more prevalent in the agriculturally richer southeast, rare in the west and absent from the poorest areas of the northeast. Most

Small Flowery Miao girls

families begin collecting for a daughter from birth—a full set, only possible for the wealthy, can weigh as much as 15 kilograms (33 pounds). The more silver she wears, the greater the prestige for herself and her family. Mothers will give their daughters part of their own collection.

When the Miao started producing silver jewellery is not known but it is thought to have begun during the Ming Dynasty (1368–1644). Before this they probably wore copper. The Miao have never been miners but purchased silver from traders, often in the form of silver coins. Today for festivals and weddings the girls wear magnificent headdresses, belts, necklaces, earrings, bracelets and rings. Many costumes incorporate silver pieces, usually attached to the back of jackets.

Miao girl from Zhouxi

Miao baby's hat with auspicious silver symbols

An old Miao fable in southeast Guizhou tells how, to separate the overlapping land and sky, a Miao hero propped up the sky with 12 silver posts. He made the moon from the remaining silver so that the earth would be bright at night. A young girl collected the shavings, among which were two crescent-shaped pieces that she used as silver horns for her head. The shavings she fashioned into combs, hairpins and a crown.

Onaments were made in the past from silver coins, melted down. From 1949 the government, to show its support and acceptance of the Miao, allocated an annual quota of silver to Miao areas, available through government shops. Much of the jewellery today is not pure silver, but it is still possible to find old pieces that are. Now, a base metal is silver-plated or an alloy is used. You will find silversmiths in many of the villages, certain of them specialize in

Typical hairstyle and ornamentation, Huaxi

this craft. Silversmiths are usually men who will practise their skill between farming tasks, unless their work is sufficiently sought after that they can employ others to work their land. Other smiths work in town, returning to their villages for the busy agricultural season.

Tang Long, outside Shidong in the southeast, is one village that produces some

Miao girl wearing her wedding crown of silver, near Kaili

(clockwise) *Black Miao girl with silver headdress, near Duyun; Bouyei woman with fashionable plucked upper forehead, near Zhenfeng; hairstyle specific to Miao men living around Congjiang; married Miao woman with everyday hairstyle and hand-woven silk headscarf, near Shidong;* (opposite page) *Dong girl dressed for a festival*

beautiful cast silver pieces. The jewellery is patterned with symbolic designs, similar to those of the embroidery of the area. Surprisingly, the *jiyu*, the mythical bird of this region's Creation Story that nurtured the eggs containing the first Miao man and the animals, does not appear often in either embroidery or jewellery designs. Girls in the Taijiang area wear silver horns representing the water buffalo, a sacred animal to the Miao. The horns may be decorated with two dragons playing with a pearl, showing the influence of Han culture on Miao designs.

The price of a necklace can be as much as one month's income for a prosperous farmer. The cost of a full silver dowry is prohibitive; most girls will wear alloys. The silversmith's daughter at Tang Long, dressed for the Sisters' Meal Festival, is a walking advertisement for her father's craft and a powerful visual indicator of her family's wealth. The silversmith recounted how, during the Cultural Revolution when silver was considered part of the old society and therefore not acceptable, he did not make any silver objects. In this period, those who had silver buried or hid it. Today most families actively save to buy silver for their daughter's dowry. Silver affords its

A baby peeps out of his embroidered baby carrier, near Liuzhi

owner some security as the girl can sell it should she or her family fall on bad times. The silversmith at Tang Long is the fifteenth generation in his family to practise this trade; one of his three sons is following in his footsteps. Of the others, one is a farmer

and the other in the army. The silver-smith feels more confident with his sons in different occupations as in this way he believes the wealth and standing of the family will be better maintained. He recognizes that it is not economically advantageous to divide the family's agricultural land into smaller plots. He does not believe in educating his three daughters, none of whom go to middle or high school, because that would mean educating them for another family clan. He views his girls as a drain on the family resources.

Children's hats are often decorated with silver images to guard against bad spirits. Images include Taoist and Buddhist gods and ancient Miao warriors and heroes, reflecting the diversity of influences on Miao culture and symbolism. Both the embroidery and the silver of children's hats, worn across all ethnic groups, are usually of the finest quality. Women in the southeast wear earrings everyday, often not of silver. Miao women can usually be distinguished by large holes in their ears and on occasion, the weight of the earrings can tear their ear

(above) *Gejia girl ready for a festival;*
(below) *Long Horned Miao mother dresses her daughter's hair*

lobes. Silver combs and other hair ornaments, torque necklaces, bracelets and rings are worn for festivals.

It is interesting to note that on market day, Miao silversmiths sell earrings and rings to Han Chinese. This has only been possible recently with the free-market economy and greater freedom for the Han to wear what they like.

Other Ethnic Groups

The diversity of ethnic groups living in the province makes it a fascinating and un-forgettable place to visit. These groups maintain independent traditions and costume styles but do share common denominators. Plan your holiday to include as many of the groups as possible.

During the Cultural Revolution traditional ways were suppressed. However, a recent resurgence of ethnic identity has led to the revival of many old customs among the middle-aged and elderly. The younger age group follow these traditions out of respect for the family, but education, contact with urban life and television are erod-ing the old customs more successfully than repression ever could. Since the reforms of the 1980s, young men have been free to move. Many become migrant labourers in the city, returning to the villages for the harvest. Consequently they enjoy a more modern outlook. The women, on the other hand, do not have as much contact with modern society and so continue to value time-honoured traditions and enjoy the festivals that serve to relieve the monotony of daily life.

The Bouyei

(Population: 2,478,100) The majority of the Bouyei of Guizhou live in three areas: Qiannan Bouyei and Miao Autonomous Prefecture in the south of the province, in the area between Anshun and Liupanshui, and near Xingyi in the southwest in two autonomous counties. Being one of the original inhabitants of southwest China, the Bouyei tend to live in the more fertile areas such as the Beipan and Nanpan river basins (North and South Plate rivers).

The Bouyei are closely related to the Zhuang, one of the earliest inhabitants of Guizhou, and their language belongs to the Zhuang-Dai branch of the Sino-Tibetan family of languages. They have no written language of their own and do not generally use the Roman script devised for them by the Chinese in 1949. Most Bouyei today will learn to speak and write Chinese at school, although the majority of the older village people neither read nor speak Chinese.

AGRICULTURE
The Bouyei live in agriculturally favourable areas of south Guizhou with a subtropi-cal climate. Those living in the lower valleys are relatively well off, growing a wide range of crops such as paddy rice, wheat, maize, sorghum, rape, vegetables and pota-toes. Cash crops include cotton, ramie, tobacco, bananas, citrus fruits, sugar cane and tea. Up to three crops a year can be grown. A common rotation is winter rape or

Miao girl from Fanpai village, near Kaili, in festival costume wheat followed by rice and vegetables. The banks between the paddy fields are planted with vegetables, notably broad beans in the spring. The few hill farmers grow millet, sorghum, buckwheat and dry rice. Oil from tung and tea trees is harvested commercially.

RELIGIOUS BELIEFS AND FUNERALS

The Bouyei remain animist and shamanist but also follow the ancestor worship of the Han Chinese, with whom they have long had close contact. Common in village centres are ancestral shrines or a large banyan tree, symbol of the village spirit. During the Spring Festival, some take a stone tied to a rope, representing an animal, to the tree to plead for assistance from the ancestors for fertility and prosperity—by dragging the stone home again their wishes will be granted by the ancestors who bring good luck. At the beginning of the 20th century some Bouyei groups were converted to Christianity. Churches with active Christian communities are still found in many areas; pictures of the Virgin Mary hang in a number of villages.

Funeral customs and after-death beliefs differ among Bouyei groups. A vivid picture of a Bouyei funeral and religious beliefs emerges from a description by Hua He, an overseas Chinese who visited Pingtang County in the Qiannan Bouyei and Miao Autonomous Prefecture in the early 1990s. The detailed painting he describes in *China Tourism* depicts the funeral procession of an old man. His children place his body in a boat which, accompanied by fish and animals and guided by a dragon, glides across the sea to a land where Bouyei horsemen, ready to fight if necessary, take the deceased under their protection. Members of the procession dance and perform acrobatics along the way to demonstrate the intelligence, ability, courage and diligence of the Bouyei people and to arouse the admiration of others. The Bouyei owe their power to their deities and ancestors. The old man is now an ancestor himself, travelling in state to visit his ancestors and the Jade Emperor in Heaven. A guard of honour in his funeral procession play the pipes and drums in a carefree manner, in striking contrast to the old man's white-clad children in mourn-

Bouyei girl with hand-woven turban and shirt, Zhenfeng area

ing. Oxen intended as sacrifice occupy the central ground. When the procession arrives at the Heavenly Bridge it is attacked by wild demons but the guards soon banish them back to the abyss. Finally, the procession arrives at the Heavenly Palace where there is a happy reunion with the ancestors of the deceased. The living and

Bouyei village surrounded by ripening rice

the dead gather round the Jade Emperor and pray together for prosperity, many progeny, a bumper harvest and peace on earth.

A markedly different set of beliefs is held by a small Bouyei village in the Liupanshui area. Here, the dead are taken immediately to a particular spot in the village because, at death, they become ghosts and no family wants a ghost in the house. They are often buried in impressive rounded graves. If a person dies before the age of 60, the ghost wanders in the mountains but should this 'wild ghost' return, it can bring bad luck and illness to the household. In this case, the shaman is called to perform a ceremony where he attempts to kill the ghost with a knife while singing special ballads and curses. However, if the deceased is over 60 years old at death, he will be invited to return to the family especially at Spring Festival as he will bring good luck.

FESTIVALS

The Bouyei celebrate many of the Han festivals including Spring Festival, May Day and the Han Ghost Festival that honours the ancestors by burning paper money and incense at home. They also celebrate their own festivals. Around the third day of the third and the sixth day of the sixth lunar months they sweep the village, symbolizing the sweeping out of evil during which the young sing love songs to each other. During the March festival, the entire village will discuss village norms and relationships, led by the unofficial village chief who is respected for his knowledge of tradition.

The **Ox Festival** is held on eighth day of the fourth lunar month when special cakes made from glutinous rice are dyed in different colours and offered to the ancestors. After the ceremony half the offerings are fed to the cattle that are rewarded for all their hard work during the year with a day of rest. Glutinous rice, pounded to a

Ground Opera (Dixi)

One priority of the Ming Dynasty (1368–1644) was the attempt to form stable borders to the south of the empire. Emperor Hong Wu (Zhu Yuanzhang), in order to put down rebellions on the borders of Yunnan, sent large numbers of troops to Guizhou where garrisons were set up. The men spent part of their time fighting and part cultivating the land to produce food for the army. Army families and entrepreneurs followed the troops to colonize the land. Han Chinese villages were set up in the Anshun area and many of these villages can be traced today by their names, which have military connotations, such as *pu* meaning garrison or *shao* meaning lookout. Often, the troops and their dependants never returned to central China and since they lived in fairly closed communities, their original language and customs have in some cases been preserved to the present day.

Troops from Nanjing settled in the Anshun area where many of the women today dress in traditional costume of that period. The people call themselves 'Nanjing people', being proud of their origins, while the locals refer to them as 'Laohan', meaning 'old Han'. These Nanjing troops specialized in a particular type of opera called Ground Opera that is still performed today by the Laohan and by some of the Bouyei people living in the area who have been influenced by this style of artistic expression. In Guizhou it is known as 'theatre on the ground' or *Dixi*. Between 200 and 300 villages in the region boast their own Dixi troupes, each of which will possess up to 100 handmade painted wooden masks, often of willow or poplar. The masks represent faces associated with the military stories that are always the subject of the operas—male warrior, old male warrior, female warrior, civil minister, painted face, clown, priest and animal faces. Masks are worn on the forehead and the face is covered with a black muslin veil. Actors are all amateur males from the villages.

The operas recreate ancient Chinese tales from the Three Kingdoms period (220–265) and the Sui (581–618) and Tang (618–907) dynasties. The performers, who know the stories by heart, are accomplished actors and very fit—local festival performances can last three to four hours a session over a two to three day period. The New Year is the season for the majority of the Ground Opera performances. Accompanied by drums and gongs, the performances are enlivened by the use of martial arts. Real weapons are used on some occasions that makes for invigorating battle scenes. Scenes, however, can be repetitive as they are played in turn to all sections of the audience, which completely surrounds the players. Other themes, such as romance, are included in the military tales to add extra dimension and appeal to the operas. Costumes are simple and consist of a loose tunic known as a *zhan pao*, to the back of which are attached four banners indicating soldier status. A military skirt, consisting of three panels wrapped around the waist, is traditionally of embroidered silk; less prosperous troupes will use cheap cotton. Charms, small bags of herbs and an embroidered purse are hung from the waist. When a character in the opera is killed by decapitation, he removes his mask. This is then picked up by the victor who places it on the floor while the 'dead' man walks off the stage. Villagers, who will know the stories well, come and go as the performance proceeds and the atmosphere is relaxed and very informal.

Both young and old attend these operas in the more remote villages, however, the urban youth are losing interest in this ancient art.

■ WHERE TO SEE
  GROUND OPERA
A troupe, especially formed so tourists can enjoy this unique style of opera that has been lost in so many parts of China, performs in the village of Caiguan, near Anshun.

All arrangements to visit the opera must be made through GZOTC or CITS.

Ground Opera performance at Caiguan

sticky consistency in a trough with a large wooden mallet, is one of the most significant festival foods. After pounding it is twisted and small pieces are filled with a mixture of chopped meat, peas, onions, vinegar and soy.

Big Year, the most impressive of the Bouyei traditional festivals, is held during the first lunar month. Villagers dressed as a lion and dragons perform an intricate dance led by a masked man. Each household hopes the lion and one of the dragons will visit their home as it will bring good luck. To encourage the visit, they wrap money in red paper ready to give to the animals. The young take the opportunity to sing to each other and the hosts prepare steamed glutinous rice, rice cakes filled with sugar and sweet rice wine.

Ground Opera (Dixi) is very popular among the Bouyei people and is performed during the New Year. Bouyei Ground Opera players often visit other ethnic group's festivals for fun and to perform for the crowds. Traditional operas from Chinese history are staged using the Han language. The Bouyei of the southwest in particular also perform their own operas based on local folk tales. During festivals, these stories can continue for several days.

COURTSHIP AND MARRIAGE

Young people mix freely at the markets and fairs and the unmarried often sing to each other, signalling the beginning of a courtship. In the low work season, the festivals and family get-togethers provide an opportunity for the young to continue their courtship. Each village will have its own set of melodic tunes and the girls invent appropriate words to sing to each guest as they offer him a drink. He must then reply in song before he can accept. Replies should rhyme, be clever and amusing to entertain the gathering of family and friends. Both boys and girls express their feelings strongly and openly. Singers must be quick-witted with their replies—the songs are a test of each others intelligence. Although good looks are appreciated, the value placed on antiphonal singing in the Bouyei culture is such that a village girl would find it difficult to get a husband if she could not sing. Courting by song often continues while working in the fields. Even the urbanized Bouyei often sing to each other in the parks of Guiyang on a Sunday. Singing is a lifelong passion for these people. An example of antiphonal singing follows, the girl begins by singing to the visitor and he replies:

Oh, little brother, you haven't been to our village for such a long time, the path must be very weedy.

It's true and I am surprised to see all the girls grown up and all so beautiful and sweet.

Another way for a girl to show attraction for a particular boy during certain festivals is to throw him a ball of silk strips that she has made herself. If he finds the girl attractive, he will seek her out and courtship will continue with singing playing a major role. When two young people decide they would like to marry, they approach their families for permission. The Bouyei have been influenced by Han society and so arranged marriages also occur. However, there is a choice to break off such childhood engagements. A villager stated that today girls are chosen for their beauty, singing ability, educational achievements, weaving and embroidery work and, in the countryside, for their agrarian skills.

On the wedding day, all the relatives go to the groom's family house. The groom's family delegate an unmarried girl to lead the way to the bride's home. They set a table outside her house and are only allowed to enter if everyone is singing. The groom makes an offering of money and is then allowed to take the girl home. After three days the bride returns to her family. If she is below marriageable age she is allowed to return home without consummating the marriage. In the past, a bride would return to her husband only for festival occasions or to assist with the rice planting. Once pregnant, she would live permanently with him. Nowadays, she will move in with her husband after a short stay with her family.

TEXTILE ARTS

Bouyei women are highly skilled at weaving and batik. Many women still weave cotton and hemp for their own costumes. An unusual finishing technique is used near Zhenfeng at a village specializing in dyeing. After dyeing with indigo, the cloth is given a lustrous shine by being placed under a huge stone that is rocked by the dyer standing on it, thus beating the cloth. This same process is used near Duyun in a

Bouyei village with tobacco-drying house in foreground

BOUYEI STONE ARCHITECTURE   Carey Vail

Nestled into the side of a hill, in the midst of lush valleys and rolling peaks, is a small Bouyei village. Within the rough rubble enclosure, narrow stone alleys lead between the houses, built close together in layers up the slope, and stone steps curve up the steepest parts of the hill. A stream gurgles past thick green bamboos and a giant banyan tree that breathes history and strength. Generations have sat in the shade of this tree, resting on stone benches smoothed by time to gossip, rest from the toil of the day and to survey their carefully-tended fields in front of the village. Children play, their laughter filling the air; chickens and dogs straggle the streets; women sit at their doorsteps carefully applying wax in intricate designs onto white hand-woven cotton to produce the batik needed to embellish their traditional costume.

Laboriously cut from the hill slope and protected by its outer wall, this village is typical of many built over the centuries by the skilled craftsmen and masons of the Bouyei tribes. Like all rural dwellers of the province, the Bouyei live mainly in small self-sufficient farming communities, growing vegetables and raising livestock within the confines of their village while reserving the flat fertile valley floor for rice and other staples.

Guizhou is mostly composed of soluble carbonate rocks, in particular karst limestone that is dissected by joints and fissures and is riddled with caves, underground streams, gulleys and peaks. Farming has always been a

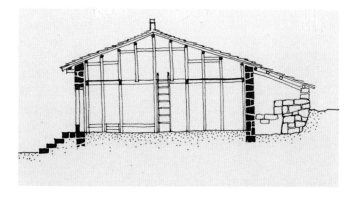

Elevation of Bouyei stone house showing the wooden spans and columns

struggle against nature, even for this ethnic group who tend to live in the more fertile areas of southern and central Guizhou—this is the province of rocks and mountains, its soil poor and thin on the slopes. Yet the Bouyei people have found their way to living in harmony with nature and with their surroundings, making the best possible use of their environment. Stone, in pleasing natural tones of cream, grey or red, serves a multitude of purposes and provides the most basic of life's necessities: shelter and defence.

The Bouyei have made themselves masters of the rocky earth and have evolved an ingenious and economical process for building. A hill slope is dug to provide a flat area; earth is removed and the stone lodged in the ground is cut out and saved for construction. Houses are timber-framed and clad with stone to provide protection and durability. They can be one- or two-storeys; some are designed with two storeys to the front and a single storey at the back. The timber frame normally consists of eight columns and seven spans. Columns are about 20 centimetres (8 inches) in diameter

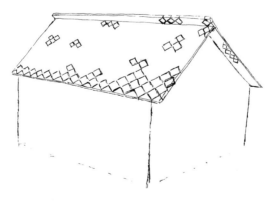

(above and below) *Stone roofing tiles*

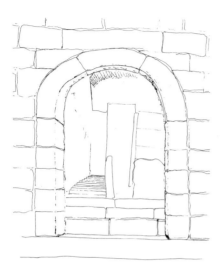

*Stone archway and stairs leading up
the alley behind*

and stand directly on the rock floor.

The houses, which are generally spacious, are positioned near a water source—apart from daily needs, a readily available water supply is vital for washing out the wax during the important process of batik. Ample room is needed for the living quarters, commonly the central room with bedrooms leading off to either side; for traditional crafts such as weaving and dyeing cloth; for housing livestock, usually in the lower storey; and for storing crops and agricultural equipment. Since no damp-proofing is installed in these houses, the ground floor can feel rather humid and the large attic, a consistent feature of this style of building, proves invaluable for storing crops dry.

Roofing material is obtained from limestone slabs. One style of roofing uses slabs from 10 centimetres (4 inches) and upwards in length of varying width, laid up the slope of the roof from eave to ridge. A second style makes use of square slabs of approximately 50 by 50 centimetres (20 by 20 inches) laid diagonally. One side of the roof is laid half a slab taller than the other, giving rise to a distinctive silhouette and acting to waterproof the roof by preventing rain from falling between the join. A half bamboo tube under the eaves serves as a gutter.

Stone walls are constructed from square or triangular blocks of hewn limestone or dark grey slate, or from rubble masonry. Slate slabs from 1 to 20 centimetres (0.5 to 8 inches) in width are often used to face the walls of public buildings that may be built up to five storeys high.

The Bouyei use stone in a variety of other skilful and practical ways—arched and flat gateways, door frames and thresholds, windowsills and bridges. Stone water tanks keep the water fresh and cool; animals drink from stone troughs; people relax on stone benches and rest in peace for perpetuity in stone tombs. Furnaces and ovens, mills, utensils such as mortars and pestles—stored in the kitchen area in stone alcoves—and drains, monuments, pavilions and small shrines are all worked from stone. Surfaces of buildings are decorated with stone frescos or carved symbols of happiness and good fortune.

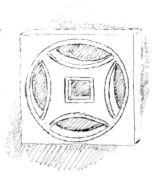

Stone window

Modern buildings are making use of the traditional materials and techniques in combination with modern technology. Recognizing the long-term advantages for the beauty of the province and for the tourist industry, some of Guizhou's tourist destinations including hotels, pavilions, teahouses, and restaurants are being built with stone to retain the harmony and natural environment of this spectacular mountain province.

Bouyei stone bridge near Huangguoshu

Shui-Miao area. A shiny cloth is valued perhaps because it indicates to the village that you have a new jacket and because, entailing much work, it is an indication of wealth. It may also repel dirt. The shine will eventually disappear as the jacket ages.

In the Libo area of south Guizhou local villages produce a fine chequered cotton cloth that is made into trousers and jackets. Surplus is sold in the markets. Recently, Bouyei weavers have been organized into a small factory producing cloth for the Japanese and Singaporean markets.

A girl with a full-time job living in town will not spend much time weaving or embroidering. However, a baby carrier is still an essential item before she can get married, even in urban areas where they are not considered fashionable. Wedding guests may present a bride with a baby carrier as a good luck token.

Women, old or young, living in the towns who do not have jobs and who have the skill produce baby carriers commercially—a common sight is women on their doorsteps sewing intently. It is interesting to note the variety and combinations of designs worked in the ethnically mixed towns.

Suggested Tour Itinerary
You can visit Bouyei groups in the Huangguoshu Waterfall area on an easy two-day trip from Guiyang. A variety of interesting Bouyei villages are accessible from Kunming (Yunnan Province)—stop at the Stone Forest, travel on to Xingyi, Xingren and Zhenfeng and finally to Guiyang via Huangguoshu.

The Dong

(Population: 1,400,300) The Dong live in the southeast in the Qiandongnan Miao and Dong Autonomous Prefecture.

The exact origins of the Dong are disputed. Many authorities believe they came from the Chang Jiang and Xi River basins but others believe they may have migrated north from Thailand.

The Dong had no written language of their own until 1958 when their spoken tongue was transcribed into the Roman script. The Dong started using the Chinese language during the Ming period (1368–1644) and today most children do so at school. The Dong belong to the Dai branch of the Sino-Tibetan language family and specifically to the Zhuang-Dong group.

Agriculture and Food
Some Dong live by the river but as much of their land is hilly or mountainous, they have built an extensive network of rice terraces. Millet, maize and sweet potatoes are

grown as staples in the poorer mountain areas. Cash crops are cotton, tobacco, rape for oil and soy bean. Fish ponds at different locations in the village provide a water supply in case of fire and fish are also reared in the rice paddy. Glutinous rice is the preferred staple. Being sticky, it can be eaten with the fingers and is taken to the fields in baskets strapped onto belts when the men and women work far from home. It is eaten with a pepper and chilli sauce. At home the Dong eat bowls of vegetables with the rice and perhaps one protein dish of pork, chicken or fish. Food is always spicy and chilli is used liberally. Glutinous rice is often dyed blue and green for festivals and is given as a present for weddings. In Rongjiang the rice is dyed black for festival meals. In common with other ethnic people, cooked glutinous rice is pounded with a wooden mallet to form cakes from the sticky mixture that is then dried. The cakes can be fried or placed over the coals to cook. They are also stored dried and when required are soaked in a bowl of water before being cooked. Rice wine is brewed for festivals. A favourite festival food is fish coated with chillies and salt and left for several years in a clay container. It is hot and spicy and much enjoyed by guests as is raw pickled pork.

Oiled tea is a speciality offered to guests, prepared by heating tea oil, puffed glutinous rice, peanuts and soya beans in a wok over the fire. The mixture is placed in individual tea bowls and tea leaves and water, boiled separately, are added. To show his politeness, a guest must drink three bowls.

ARCHITECTURE

The Dong live in villages in wooden houses two-to-four storeys high. Fir tends to be the favoured wood. To mark the birth of a child, a fir sapling is planted that on marriage is often felled to build the couple's new home. Domestic animals are kept on the ground level and the upper floors serve as living quarters. A central fireplace is surrounded by a large open space where the women weave and spin, the men make baskets and fishing nets and the family eats. The elderly are provided with bedrooms at the back of the house, usually heated.

Many villages feature large wooden drum towers of magnificent design and traditionally constructed without the use of nails. These towers serve as meeting places for the villagers, disputes are solved here, stories told and songs sung. People also meet here on festival days. In the past each tower contained a huge drum that was beaten should the village be in danger of attack. Villagers would gather at the tower with the clan head to defend the village. Villages would often boast two or three of these towers, one for each clan. You can see an example of this at Zhaoxing, 80 kilometres (50 miles) from Congjiang.

Another feature of Dong architecture is the covered wooden bridges. These are known as 'wind and rain' bridges where travellers can shelter from the elements.

(following pages) Dong village with typical drum tower and 'wind and rain' bridge, Zhaoxing

Unfortunately many of these bridges fell into disrepair or were partially destroyed during the Cultural Revolution. An extensive restoration and reconstruction programme during the 1980s has meant the bridges are once again a feature of the landscape; the best example is the Diping bridge at Rongjiang.

In the lowland areas, spectacular series of bamboo waterwheels raise the water from the river to the fields.

RELIGIOUS BELIEFS AND FUNERALS
In the past the people were animist and shamanist, believing in spirits that had to be controlled. Every village has a shaman. Despite disapproval of these ancient beliefs after 1949, traditional practices continued. The shaman is consulted when someone is ill to exorcize the evil spirit. His services are particularly in demand when someone dies. A paper boat is set afloat on the river to signify that the spirit of the dead person is released. After this the body is buried in a grave in wasteland.

The Dong follow the Han Chinese custom of ancestor worship and various of their practices such as sweeping the grave at Qing Ming (Festival to the Dead) after which a feast is held at the grave, offerings first being made to the ancestors.

FESTIVALS
The Dong use the Han lunar calendar and hold numerous festivals throughout the year giving the young an opportunity to meet boys and girls from neighbouring villages. If you plan your journey carefully, you should be able to visit at least one of their festivals.

After the main events of a festival, girls and boys sit opposite each other singing together until dawn. The next morning, dressed in their best, the girls sit under the drum towers while the boys and men persuade the girls and women to go with them to their village to continue the festivities.

Tai Guan Ren Carnival in Congjiang County coincides with the Han Chinese Spring Festival at the beginning of the first lunar month. Visitors from a neighbouring village dress up as bandits, goblins, soldiers and strange animals. A man dressed in silk as a government official is paraded through the village in a sedan chair. Everyone asks him for money and it is only when his purse is emptied that the girls clear the way for him to continue. The money is a New Year gift given by the guests to the host village. The 'government official', *Guan Ren*, is followed by girls from his village dressed in festive clothes. After the parade both villages entertain each other with songs under the drum tower. This ceremony represents the Dong people's desire for fair and equal treatment by enacting the scene of a landlord sharing out his money.

Cai Ge Tang, also in the first lunar month, is when the young sing and dance in front of the temple dedicated to their ancestral heroine, Sasui. Everyone dresses up in their finery, there are singing competitions and the lusheng pipes are played. Over a thousand years ago, Xing Ni died in a battle fighting for freedom. The Dong call her Sasui ('grandmother'). When she died, each village sent people to collect rocks from the battleground, which were buried in their own villages to become Sasui temples.

Sing-a-Song Festival is held on the third day of the third lunar month. Close to each village is a hillside traditionally chosen for this event. The young people walk up this hill, taking a picnic of glutinous rice, and girls and boys attract each other's attention by singing to each other. A girl will show her attraction for a boy by giving him a clove of garlic. If he is interested they will sing to each other, chanting to and fro in the antiphonal style.

COURTSHIP AND MARRIAGE

The Dong, like the Bouyei, are very fond of singing. They are known for their antiphonal courting songs. They also play the pipes and a guitar-like instrument. Traditionally a visitor to the village is greeted with a song. A bough is drawn across the entrance to the village and a group of women sing to the guests who must sing in return before the barrier is drawn up. The party then proceeds to the village shrine where more singing takes place and rice and pork are offered to the visitors.

The young meet each other at festivals, after which approaches are made by the boy's family to gain the girl's hand in marriage. However, under the influence of Han customs, arranged marriages are now very common. Once consent is given for a marriage, the date is set. In common with the Han Chinese, a geomancer is asked to calculate the most auspicious day for the wedding. A chicken may be killed to determine the fate of the marriage, depending on whether the chicken's eyes are open or closed when it dies. If the signs are not propitious the marriage is called off.

After the date has been set, the boy's family will bring gifts to the girl's family who in turn sends presents of cloth and embroidered shoe insoles to his family. On the wedding day the groom takes a party of girls and boys to the bride's house to collect her. There will be a large banquet and the girl will stay overnight at the groom's house before returning to stay with her parents the next morning. She goes to stay at her husband's house for the busy farming seasons to assist her new family but does not live permanently with him until she is pregnant. In some areas these traditions are no longer observed.

TEXTILE ARTS

From an early age the girls learn to spin and weave cotton that is grown in many of the Dong areas. They dye their own clothes in locally-grown indigo. This is one of the most important areas for growing and dyeing indigo in Guizhou.

There are many similarities with the processes used by the Miao but in some

areas relatively close to each other, slightly different processes are used. In a village near Rongjiang we saw indigo paste being made in wooden barrels by the river. The main season for this is July and August. Many villages dye cloth for their own use, the cotton cloth often being hand-woven from home-grown cotton. The cloth is dipped in the indigo, dried and dipped again to achieve the

Dong woman laying out indigo-dyed cloth to dry, near Congjiang

desired colour. Loom lengths are often steamed in a long thin bamboo tube. Glue extracted from boiling cowhide is rubbed on by hand, probably to fix the colour helped by the constant rinsing of excess dye in the river. Cloth is also beaten with a wooden mallet to give a shine. In areas near Congjiang we saw a similar process but no evidence of steaming. Here, the shine is achieved by hammering the length of cloth on a stone slab with a wooden mallet. After the cloth is passed through several solutions of sticky bark soaked in water, it is sometimes rubbed with wax. The indigo has a red sheen, possibly achieved by applying animal blood but more likely the natural indigo colour brought out by good dyeing. Another method to obtain a beautiful shine is to paint on persimmon juice, dry the cloth and then apply egg white. Clothes subject to this process are called 'egg clothes'.

Many of the Dong live in remote areas and the girls still wear traditional costume daily. Styles vary with the area but jackets and trousers or pleated skirts are common. Some Dong still elaborately embroider the sleeves, the front of the jackets and an edging on the trousers but machine-made braid is increasingly used. The most exquisite embroidery is usually found on baby carriers.

Girls adorn themselves with silver ornaments such as chains, bracelets, hairpins and combs but they do not usually wear the elaborate silver crowns of the Miao.

Suggested Tour Itinerary

A visit to the Dong area is highly recommended, particularly for their outstanding local architecture. Tours can be arranged by specialist agents. You can spend four to seven days travelling from Guiyang to Kaili, Rongjiang, Congjiang, Zhaoxing and finally to Sanjiang and Guilin (Guangxi) passing through Dong areas.

Dong man dressed in indigo-dyed jacket and turban

The Shui

(Population: 322,600) The Shui live in south and southeast Guizhou near the towns of Libo, Dushan, Duyun, Rongjiang and the Leigong Mountain area.

The Shui originated from the Xi Jiang (Pearl River) basin in Guangxi Autonomous Region and migrated north in the Qin Dynasty (221–207 BC) and the early centuries AD. Others believe they may have come from as far as Fujian Province in the east. Their language belongs to the Dai group, a subdivision of the Sino-Tibetan linguistic group. There is no script for their spoken language but village shamans have created a series of pictograms that illustrate the various shamanistic practices. These old manuscripts are being deciphered by academics. Since 1949 the Shui have been pressed into going to school where they are taught in Chinese.

AGRICULTURE AND FOOD
The Shui are farming people. In the lowland they grow rice as a staple, some vegetables including potatoes, and keep pigs and chicken. Fish are kept in ponds or in the paddy fields. Groups living in the hills where irrigation is not possible grow maize and millet. Traditionally, the Shui grew glutinous rice as a staple, but as this is a low-yield crop that needs more water and has a longer growth period, they have switched to high-yield paddy rice. A small quantity of glutinous rice is still grown for festivals. Other crops include wheat, rape for oil, ramie and cotton.

The Shui eat rice and vegetables on a daily basis with very small amounts of protein but enjoy entertaining with a rich high-protein meal to demonstrate their wealth and to honour their guests. A typical meal for visitors might start with chicken or fish stock boiled in a wok with garlic and ginger. To this is added bean curd, chopped pork, sliced liver and kidney, pieces of fish and bean shoots. Suspended above the wok, a dish of dried chilli, chopped onions, soy sauce, vinegar and stock serves as the communal dip. A sauce made from ground chilli and vinegar is also popular. Glutinous rice, eaten with the fingers, maize spirits and rice wines accompany the meal.

VILLAGE LIFE
Each village is led by a Party cadre and an unofficial, well-respected tribal chief who has an understanding and knowledge of local tradition. He must be eloquent and diplomatic so that he can negotiate with ease for he will be expected to settle domestic disputes. He will officiate at wedding banquets, making long speeches to introduce each family. Debating and the art of oratory are highly prized skills in Shui society. The loser in a debate is forced to drink large quantities of rice or maize spirit.

Women help in the fields, carry out all domestic tasks and are excellent at spinning, weaving and embroidery, the latter particularly.

Religious Beliefs and Funerals

Funerals are organized by the tribal chief and the village shaman. In the past these involved animal sacrifices and a complicated system of rituals and taboos. Funerals today have been simplified but retain many elements of the Shui's ceremonial rules. For example, when a married woman dies, her relatives are informed and must come to see her body. They are prohibited from eating animal flesh or fat until she is buried but may eat fish, bean curd and vegetables. She will be buried on an auspicious day that must be an odd number in the calendar. The coffin is made from wood and must not contain any metal as this is unlucky. The body is dressed in the finest clothes and a silver coin is placed in the mouth to help the deceased buy water on the journey back to the ancestors.

The Shui believe each person has 12 souls that should return to their origins on death. Bad souls will plague the living as ghosts but good souls will protect. A tremendous effort is made to follow all taboos correctly to ensure the family will not be troubled by these bad souls.

Festivals

The Shui play the lusheng pipes and are particularly adept at bronze drumming on festival occasions. The Sandu area was home to some of the oldest Shui bronze drums. However, during the Great Leap Forward campaign launched in 1958, hundreds or perhaps thousands of these bronze drums were melted down in small blast furnaces on the communes to produce iron and steel.

As villages become better off in the 1990s, these drums are gradually being replaced. Two people are required to play the drum: one to beat out the tune, the other to move the bowl at the rear in and out.

The **Duan Festival** is one of the Shui's most significant as it celebrates the life-giving harvest. The date of the festival varies with the harvest and across regions, but is normally held during the tenth lunar month on an appropriate lucky animal day. An added complication in calculating the date of this festival is the Shui's own calendar that requires festivals to fall on specific auspicious days.

The festival celebrates the birth of the Shui new year and pays respects to the ancestors. On the eve of the festival, each household catches a large fish that is then stuffed with ginger, glutinous rice and peppers. Vegetables, bean curd, rice and fruit is also prepared for a big family banquet in honour of the ancestors. No meat is eaten and no oil is used in the cooking. The following day is considered a village holiday and one of the favourite activities is horse racing. A huge brass drum is beaten to symbolize the beating out of the old year and the ringing in of the new. On these occasions the women and men eat separately. The women, dressed in their festival finery, are very active in the playing of the drum.

Song Festival or *Jie Mao*, held only in certain areas, is for the young men and women from different villages to meet together, dress in their best clothes and sing antiphonal love songs to each other while wandering a selected hillside. This takes place during the fifth or sixth lunar month. Occasionally a love match is formed and betrothal gifts are sent. However, this is unusual as most Shui marriages are arranged. Without family consent, the couple could not survive economically as they would receive no help from families and would have no position in their society.

MARRIAGE

Like the Miao, Shui girls wear silver ornaments for festivals and weddings. Silver represents the family wealth and each woman will own a collection. On marriage a girl's family provides the wedding dress and silver bracelets, the boy's family gives her a silver necklace. Depending on family resources, the bride may be given her mother's silver or new silver is purchased from silversmiths.

SUGGESTED TOUR ITINERARY

You can make an interesting circular tour of the Shui area from Guiyang staying at Duyun, Dushan, Libo, Sandu and back to Guiyang. If you wish to extend your tour, stay at Kaili before returning to Guiyang.

The Yi

(Population: 707,400) The Yi are the largest ethnic group in southwest China, but in Guizhou they are restricted to the Bijie area, Liupanshui and small communities around Anshun.

The word 'Yi' has been applied to this group since 1949. Prior to this they were known as Nosu or, by the Han Chinese, as Luoluo, a derogatory term. *Luoluo*, originally meaning 'tiger', was used by the Yi people themselves until the end of the Ming period (1368–1644) when the Han added a prefix to the written character that altered its meaning to 'savage animal'. The Yi, not surprisingly, strongly objected and dropped the use of the name among themselves. In 1949, the Chinese gave them a character for 'Yi' meaning 'rice and silk held in a container' as an indication that after Liberation, their life would become more prosperous and they would be respected. The term 'luoluo' is never used today.

The Yi were originally nomads and migrated over 7,000 years ago from Qinghai, Gansu and Shaanxi provinces to the present-day Yunnan, Sichuan and Guizhou. They turned to agriculture and were living around Lake Dianchi in Yunnan Province by the second century BC. They had their own state that lasted until AD 937.

Shui people in everyday dress, near Duyun

The Fall and Rise of a Black Yi Landlord

A three-metre (ten-foot) tall memorial tombstone in the Weining area, embellished with angels, a cross and a bible, mark the burial place of a Black Yi landlord who had been particularly enlightened for his time. He died during the Cultural Revolution (1966–1976) when it had not been possible to erect a memorial and so in recent years his family clubbed together to pay for this, one of the largest and most ornate tombstones in the area.

His granddaughter, a 23-year old woman living in Guiyang, related the story of this man and his family. Her parents were both schoolteachers in Weining, tall, well-educated and highly respected as a family. Her grandfather had ensured that he and all his children received further education at colleges or universities, he himself at the Chengdu Medical College. He had been converted to Christianity at the beginning of the century and continued his studies at a seminary, after which he returned to Weining to lead the local church and to set up the Chong Shi Primary and Middle School with the help of an English missionary. The family prospered, until in 1949 their lands were taken from them and redistributed to the peasants. The family survived due to its acceptance of and belief in the new socialist principles; several members became respected Party cadres. However, the family fell again under the onslaught of the Cultural Revolution with its renewed vigour in purging and punishing the old system. By the 1980s, the family had regained its standing, and the grandfather was rehabilitated posthumously. He can now be fully recognized by those in his family and community and can be freely honoured for his work and his tolerant, forward-thinking attitudes.

The Yi have their own spoken and written language, the latter being the property of the shamans. Manuscripts in the old Yi script, dating back to the 13th century, include works of history, literature, medicine and genealogies of the ruling families. Characters engraved on tortoiseshells from the Shang period (16th–11th centuries BC) found in Shaanxi Province are similar to those used in the old Yi script and it is speculated that a Yi language could date from this time. Yi belongs to the Tibeto-Burman linguistic groups, however, a number of distinct local dialects exists. Today in Guizhou only approximately 30 per cent of the Yi people speak their own language, the rest use Chinese.

The Yi, who were farmers, had a well-developed social structure. Landlords accounted for 5 per cent of the population; the remainder rented their land and paid for it in kind. The peasants in Guizhou were very poor, living in mountainous areas where agriculture was difficult. In the Liangshan mountains of south Sichuan, where there is a major concentration of over 1.5 million, the Yi had a particularly well-defined social system that continued until 1949 and spread over the border into northwest Guizhou. The Black Yi, the highest rank, were the aristocrats and relatively well-off landowners.

Intermarriage with the lower class, the White Yi, was forbidden. This group had no rights to land and could be bought, sold or killed, being regarded by the Black Yi as mere 'talking tools'. The old system broke down slowly but even today, some people are recognized as coming from the older aristocratic classes. There is no advantage now in belonging to this class, which was severely criticised in the various campaigns after 1949. People from this group are now teased and are mockingly called princes and princesses.

AGRICULTURE

Many of the Yi today continue to farm, others have been integrated into the towns and have taken up industrial jobs. The urban Yi can no longer be recognized as an independent ethnic group. Those remaining in the countryside live mainly in hilly and mountainous areas and are more traditional in their ways. Farming has improved since 1949 but, in the harsh mountainous areas of Bijie, the staples are still maize, buckwheat and potatoes. Flocks of sheep and goats are kept in the poor mountainous areas, particularly around Weining. Experts from New Zealand have recently been invited to advise on reseeding pastures—grass seed is brought in from New Zealand and pastures are seeded from the air. The animal stock has been improved with the introduction of new breeds and quality wool is now being produced in the Weining area. Improved farming techniques have meant the farmers in the valleys now grow rice and tobacco as a cash crop. Hemp, grown extensively in the past and used as the chief fibre used for cloth, is still grown in remote areas along with ramie. Ready-woven woollen and cotton textiles from the the towns supplement local supplies.

A VILLAGE VISIT

The Yi are a very hospitable people and welcome guests with great ceremony at the entrance to the village. On a typical visit to a Yi village, cornet-like instruments called *suona* are blown and a drum is beaten enthusiastically. The host serves the guest with a strong alcoholic maize liquor, often in a ram's horn. The guests are then escorted to the village, ushered into the host's house and plied with the best food and drink the family can offer. Snacks are offered before the meal, which commonly starts with a drinking ceremony.

In some villages guests must drink the liquor through a straw from a central

Honoured Guests

Everything was strange, from mud-walled barn and dancing shadows high up in the darkness, to shuffling retainers and grunting animals who shared the house with us. One man was cleaning his rifle while another sat plucking his beard hair by hair with fine forceps. Preoccupied as I was with watching, a sudden scuffle and shrill squealing alarmed me and yet was half expected, as they caught a passing pig and holding it down on the ground by the light of a flaring firebrand plunged a knife into its neck. I protested, but I might have saved myself the trouble. In spite of all my stipulations Chao and Aku did no more than remonstrate a moment with the hostess. She was adamant.

'Of course a company like this should be fêted. What would everyone say if they were denied the feast that the occasion demands?'

'Never mind,' they said to me, 'it's only a little one.'

But in the morning the inevitable present in return had to be produced; on Chao's advice, two small bolts of calico, three face-cloths, and some thread, needles and combs.

As we talked the pig was dipped whole into a cauldron of boiling water, scalded all over, and transferred to a bamboo mat. The 'slaves of the hearth' tried scraping it with a stick and knife but seemed to prefer their own finger-nails. They managed to remove most of the encrusted dirt before the fire was built up to white heat and the carcase held over it and turned slowly till its bristles had been singed and the skin toasted. Cold water was then poured over it, and back on the floor it was cut open, disembowelled and hacked into fist-sized chunks. The heart and liver were put in the ashes at the edge of the fire and turned once or twice before they were removed, flicked free of excess ash, and with deep ceremonial bows presented by a White to me first, then Aku, and the others of our party.

While the flames were bright it was essential to behave politely, and we followed Chao's instructions to scrape off the ashes as best we could, and enjoy the delicatessen with which we had been honoured. But the flesh, half-raw, and anyway, alive so few minutes before, I found revolting. With the greatest effort I controlled my retching and took a bite. The surface half-inch was well cooked, but deeper it was tough and juicy. Fortunately by the time I had devoured the ashy surface layer and was wondering how to deal with the raw centre, the fire sank for a brief moment, and one desperate flick sent what was left into the shadows, to a waiting dog.

Meanwhile the chunks of pork were tipped into the cauldron and brought to the boil. We had heard about the Nosu custom of adding cold water when the meat was ready, and managed to persuade them on this first occasion to spare us the prospect of typhoid fever, dysentery and all the ills of water-borne infection. But never again. Every day for the next week we ate in Nosu style, as unhygienically as could be, and came to no harm. The other chiefs with whom we stayed, would not allow the flavour to be 'spoiled' by our new-fangled notions.

When the meat was done to their satisfaction, the retainers using three-foot ladles lifted it into large wooden bowls, painted yellow, red and black in the gayest variety of patterns, and offered it to us. As they did so the hostess rose to find some lacquered spoons. To my astonishment, from the shadows where they had been gathering, silently and unobserved, two or three score of White men, women and children stood up, and paused until she was seated again beside the fire before they sat to await their turn to eat. It was a sight we soon became accustomed to, but never did the sense of the romantic lessen. In that 'mediaeval' atmosphere, when the laird or his lady moved, born aristocrats however unwashen, gliding with head erect and pleated skirts sweeping rhythmically at heel, it always stirred my blood to hear the swish of movement and to see the hall-full of retainers rise in a wave while they passed.

The guests and household separated into groups of four or five, around big bowls of rice and soup and meat, and each man with a spoon in the right hand, for rice and soup, and a chunk of meat held in the left hand, gnawed and ate regardless of the others. We were ravenous. Two meals a day was bad enough without exercise, but after walking and riding even ten miles, no meal however crude could be resisted. The meat was no better cooked than the liver had been, but after our initiation it was easier to be philosophical, and before long we were tearing at the dripping flesh with full enjoyment. As we finished the retainers gathered up all that was left, and with their hands divided up the heap of remnants, by now cold and doubly repulsive, for the serfs to share.

It was midnight before activity had dwindled enough to make sleep possible. But when we unrolled our bedding the excitement started up again. All the Nosu simply lay down where they chose, beside the fire or in a group where they could smoke their opium undisturbed.

A J Broomhall, Strong Man's Prey, 1953

barrel. After returning to the table, they are encouraged to consume even more alcohol by the prettiest girls in the family who sing a cheerful, catchy drinking song. Regular toasts are made throughout the meal when the best meats, including goat which is very popular, and glutinous rice is served. Friends chat and gossip. When the guests depart the entire village sees them off, led by all the dignitaries of the community to the edge of the village, all the while singing a repetitive catchy melody.

RELIGIOUS BELIEFS AND FUNERALS

Many of the Yi are still animist and very superstitious. They have been influenced by Buddhism, Taoism, Christianity and particularly by the theory of balance and opposites as expressed by Yin and Yang—earth and heaven, black and white.

Each village in the countryside will have a shaman, generally a working farmer, whose job it is to control bad spirits. There are two types of shaman. The first cannot read Yi and will learn his skills from village elders and other shamans. He is in charge of driving away evil spirits and cultivating good ones. The second is well-educated and can read the Yi chronicles and explain the group's history. He is highly respected as a teacher. Both shamans take part in funerals so a balance is achieved.

At death the Yi look forward to their spirit returning to the original ancestral homeland to join their loved ones. Originally a dead body was left to petrify on a tree before burial. This practice has been discontinued and now bodies, after certain ceremonies are performed, are buried in graves in the open country. A dance is sometimes performed entailing a simple crossing of one foot over the other to represent stamping on the worms in the body, thus allowing the spirit to be released.

In this matriarchal society the most important family representative is the maternal uncle. This uncle, family members and friends are invited to the funeral to which all guests must bring something for the feast—an ox, pigs, chickens, rice, liquor and salt for the cooking. The animals are killed and the feast is prepared for the invited guests. Before this, however, the three souls of the dead person are released in a ceremony officiated by two shamans. One soul

Yi people making music

goes to the ancestors, the second stays at the grave site and the third goes to the ancestral altar. The shamans give instructions to the family who then perform a ritual that includes weaving back and forth in a long line to show the journey the soul must take to return to the ancestors. The path is marked with white lime and fires are held high on bamboo poles to help the soul of the deceased find its way. This ritual is common to the area around Pan Xian and has close similarities to some Miao beliefs.

Traditional Yi costume

FESTIVALS

The numerous Yi festivals are determined by the Chinese lunar calendar and incorporate many Han festivals. Both men and women today tend to wear Han clothing but for festivals and weddings the women wear traditional costume.

Torch Festival, celebrated around the 20th of the sixth lunar month, has its origins in a wrestling match between two strong men, one in heaven and the other on earth. When the strong man of the sky was defeated he let loose swarms of locusts to destroy the crops. To prevent this damage, the Yi lit torches to drive out the pests. Entertainment at this torch-lit festival includes horse racing, bullfighting, archery, wrestling, singing and dancing.

Ancestor Worship is an integral part of life in the Wumeng Mountain area and a local tale explains the significance of the family altar. A long time ago the village was destroyed by flooding and the villagers built a boat to take refuge. Eventually this boat ran aground on dry land and was held fast by the grass. In memory of this event, villagers make twists of grass to place on the family shrine, one for each generation who has lived there since the time of the flood.

The family shrine is kept in the home of the eldest son and rice is offered to it after a good harvest. Ceremonies honouring the ancestors are often held at Spring Festival. Many rural villagers hang photographs of Mao Ze Dong near the family shrine, showing their continued allegiance to him for rescuing them, as they see it, from the bad old ways.

Marriage

Prior to 1949, marriages were always arranged by the family because of the Yi's strong class structure, but young people today, particularly those working in the towns, are beginning to choose their own marriage partners. Tradition is still followed in rural areas where arranged marriages are common. The partner of choice for a girl is her maternal uncle's son. Black and White Yi groups still rarely intermarry, although there is an upper class within White Yi society that can, on occasion, marry a Black Yi.

Suggested Tour Intinerary

You can visit Yi villages by travelling from Guiyang to the Shuicheng area, where visits to selected villages can be arranged. An interesting 10–12 day itinerary to both Yi and Miao villages starts at Kunming (Yunnan Province), stopping at the Stone Forest, then to Pan Xian in Guizhou. The adventurous might like to visit the coal mine at Tucheng before setting off for Shuicheng and Weining. You can return to Guiyang via Shuicheng and Liuzhi.

Areas around Bijie and Weining have only recently opened to foreign visitors and many remain closed, so check first with GZOTC or CITS whether they are accessible before planning to visit them.

The Yao

(Population: 18,000) The Yao live in the south of Guizhou in close proximity to Shui villages. You can visit Yao villages in the Libo area. They are closely related to the Miao and probably had common ancestors, both belonging to the Miao-Yao branch of the Sino-Tibetan language family. The Yao lived in western Hunan during the Qin and Han periods (221 BC–AD 220). Originally they had their own language but today most speak Miao, Dong or Chinese. Yao is spoken only by a few today. Before 1949 they had no written language of their own but kept records of significant events by carving notches on wood or bamboo slips. They have used Chinese characters since at least the Ming period (1368–1648). One feature of a Yao village is the stone pillar that records all marriages, thus ensuring there is no intermarriage.

The name 'Yao' was officially given to them in 1949. Before this at least 30 names were ascribed to them based on their dress. Local people still know them by these old names, for example near Libo they are Green, White or Gowan (daisy) Yao. Two thousand years ago when they were living around Changsha (Hunan Province) they were called the Wuling tribes and later Moyao. The famous poet, Du Fu (712–770) wrote, 'the Moyaos shoot wild geese with bows made from mulberry trees'.

The Yao celebrate several of their own festivals and singing to the accompaniment of drums, gongs and suona horns is an indispensable part of their life.

AGRICULTURE

Originally hunters, the Yao turned to agriculture in the tenth century but continued some hunting. Their agricultural life is similar to the other groups in Guizhou but they specialize in secondary occupations such as collecting edible fungi, star anise and medicinal herbs. They also make charcoal if there are forests nearby. The Yao often live on steep mountainsides and still practice a slash and burn economy, growing dry rice in some areas. Because slash and burn causes erosion, this practice is being stopped by the government. The Yao stand out for their 'singing while digging'. During the spring ploughing, 20 to 30 households work together on each other's land. A young man stands in the field beating a drum to encourage the rhythm of work. Rice, maize, sweet potatoes and taro are the staple crops and they enjoy glutinous rice. They grow and smoke tobacco and a daily necessity is oily tea. Tea leaves are fried in oil, boiled into a thick, salty soup and mixed with puffed rice or soy beans. This is drunk for breakfast or lunch. Banquet delicacies include pickled birds, beef and mutton.

MARRIAGE

A boy will court a girl by going to her house and pushing a stick through a hole in the wall. If the girl takes it, this is an invitation for him to enter the house where he will sing to her. If a couple decides to marry, they will ask their parents to make wedding arrangements. The bridegroom's family must pay a bride price in cash and give expensive gifts to the bride's family.

TEXTILE ARTS

Western clothes are now the norm for the majority of Yao who no longer wear traditional costume. However, girls still learn to weave and embroider and make their own costumes for festivals and weddings.

The Tujia

(Population: 1,028,200) The Tujia are found in northeast Guizhou on the border with Hunan at an elevation of 400–1,500 metres (1,312–4,921 feet). You can visit Tujia villages outside Tongren but no specific arrangements are made for tourists. Some believe the Tujia's original homeland was in Guizhou Province, others that they came from Jiangxi Province in the Tang Dynasty (618–907). Certainly by the

Five Dynasties period (907–960) they were a distinct group living in northeast Guizhou and west Hunan.

The Tujia belong to the Tibeto-Burman branch of the Sino-Tibetan language family, but it is only in the most remote regions that Tujia is spoken today. The vast majority speak the language of the Han Chinese with whom they have

Tujia peasants carrying logs up Fanjing

been assimilated since the Ming period (1368–1644) when they were sent as soldiers to fight Japanese pirates on the east coast of China. They were recognized officially as a distinct ethnic group in 1950.

The Tujia are farmers and foresters although many live in the towns and work alongside the Han Chinese in small factories and collectives. They have adopted many Han customs including Taoism, ancestor worship and most of their festivals. The Tujia maintain some of their own traditional dances and folk songs and are talented at singing and composing.

Traditional costume is only worn in the most remote areas where the skills of embroidery and weaving continue.

The Gelao

(Population: 430,500) The majority of the Gelao in China live in western Guizhou near Zhijin, Qianxi, Liuzhi and Zunyi.

The Gelao are descended from one of the strongest tribes in China, the Yelang, and lived in the Sichuan area during the Han period (206 BC–AD 220). From the Yuan Dynasty (1271–1368) their homelands were controlled by the Han Chinese. During the Ming Dynasty (1368–1644) they were called Liao and were ruled by tribal chiefs.

The Gelao belong to the Sino-Tibetan linguistic group but most speak Chinese as the strong local dialects that developed resulted in them not being able to understand each other. For the most part, the Gelao have been assimilated into the culture of the Han Chinese.

TRADITIONAL FESTIVALS IN GUIZHOU

Festival	Minority Group	No of Partici- pants	Place	Date			
				1994	1995	1996	1997
Lusheng Festival	Miao	10,000	Kaili and Huangping	10–12 Feb	31 Jan– 2 Feb	19–21 Feb	15–17 Feb
Lusheng Festival	Miao	20,000	Villages around Kaili	12–14 Feb	2–4 Feb	21–23 Feb	7–9 Feb
Lusheng Festival	Miao	12,000	Lengshuigou, Guanyingshan, Lushan, Kaili	13–14 Feb	3–4 Feb	22–23 Feb	10–13 Feb
Lusheng Festival	Miao	5,000	Wanchao, Ma'anshan Kaili	19–21 Feb	9–11 Feb	28 Feb –1 Mar	16–18 Feb
Lusheng Festival	Miao	10,000	Lushan, Da- fang Dong, Kaili	19–21 Feb	9–11 Feb	28 Feb –1 Mar	16–18 Feb
Lusheng Festival	Miao	10,000	Huaxi, Guiyang	18 Feb	8 Feb	27 Feb	15 Feb
Lusheng Festival	Miao	5,000	Zhouxi, Kaili	20–24 Feb	10–14 Feb	29 Feb –4 Mar	16–20 Feb
Lusheng Festival	Miao	30,000	Zhouxi, Kaili	20–24 Feb	10–14 Feb	29 Feb –4 Mar	16–20 Feb
Lusheng Festival	Miao	5,000	Zhouxi, Wengdi, Kaili	20–21 Feb	10–11 Feb	29 Feb –1 Mar	17–18 Feb

Date						Activities
1998	1999	2000	2001	2002	2003	
5–7 Feb	24–26 Feb	13–15 Feb	1–3 Feb	20–23 Feb	9–11 Feb	Lusheng dance, antiphonal singing, horse race
28–30 Jan	16–18 Feb	5–7 Feb	24–26 Jan	12–14 Feb	1–3 Feb	Lusheng dance, antiphonal singing, horse race, bullfight
31 Jan –2 Feb	19–21 Feb	8–10 Feb	27–29 Feb	15–17 Feb	4–6 Feb	Lusheng dance, antiphonal singing, horse race
6–8 Feb	25–27 Feb	14–16 Feb	2–4 Feb	21–23 Feb	10–12 Feb	Lusheng dance, bullfight, horse race
6–8 Feb	25–27 Feb	14–16 Feb	2–4 Feb	21–23 Feb	10–12 Feb	Lusheng dance, bullfight, horse race
5 Feb	24 Feb	13 Feb	1 Feb	20 Feb	9 Feb	Lusheng dance, antiphonal singing, bullfight
6–10 Feb	25–29 Feb	14–18 Feb	2–6 Feb	21–25 Feb	10–15 Feb	Lusheng dance, antiphonal singing, bullfight
6–10 Feb	25–29 Feb	14–18 Feb	2–6 Feb	21–25 Feb	10–15 Feb	Lusheng dance, beating bronze drum, bullfight
7–8 Feb	26–27 Feb	15–16 Feb	3–4 Feb	22–23 Feb	11–12 Feb	Lusheng dance, bullfight, horse race

Festival	Minority Group	No of Partici-pants	Place	Date			
				1994	1995	1996	1997
Lusheng Festival	Miao	5,000	Zhouxi, Xing-guang, Kaili	21–22 Feb	11–12 Feb	1–2 Mar	18–19 Feb
Lusheng Festival	Miao	5,000	Qingman, Kaili	22–23 Feb	12–13 Feb	2–3 Mar	19–20 Feb
Lusheng Festival	Miao	5,000	Wanchao, Matian, Kaili	23 Feb	13 Feb	3 Mar	20 Feb
Lusheng Festival	Miao	5,000	Panghai, Wan-shui, Kaili	24–26 Feb	14–16 Feb	4–6 Mar	21–23 Feb
Ground Opera Festival	Bouyei	20,000	Huaxi, Guiyang	24 Feb	15 Feb	4 Mar	21 Feb
Dragon Lantern Festival	Miao	10,000	Taijiang, Shidong	24 Feb	15 Feb	4 Mar	21 Feb
Lusheng Festival	Miao	5,000	Wanchao, Sanjiang, Kaili	25 Feb	15 Feb	5 Mar	22 Feb
Lusheng Festival	Miao	30,000	Zhouxi, Kaili	25–27 Feb	15–17 Feb	5–7 Mar	22–24 Feb
Lusheng Festival	Miao	20,000	Wanchao, Longchang, Kaili	26 Feb	16 Feb	6 Mar	23–24 Feb
Sanyuesan ('3.3')	Dong, Miao	10,000	Baojing, Zhenyuan	13 Apr	2 Apr	20 Apr	9 Apr

Date						Activities
1998	1999	2000	2001	2002	2003	
8–9 Feb	27–28 Feb	16–17 Feb	4–5 Feb	23–24 Feb	12–13 Feb	Lusheng dance, bullfight, horse race
9–10 Feb	28–29 Feb	17–18 Feb	5–6 Feb	24–25 Feb	13–14 Feb	Lusheng dance, beating bronze drum
10 Feb	1 Mar	18 Feb	6 Feb	25 Feb	14 Feb	Lusheng dance, bullfight, horse race, antiphonal singing
11–13 Feb	2–5 Mar	19–21 Feb	7–9 Feb	26–28 Feb	15–17 Feb	Lusheng dance, bullfight, horse race
11 Feb	2 Mar	19 Feb	7 Feb	26 Feb	15 Feb	Performance of Ground Opera
11 Feb	2 Mar	19 Feb	7 Feb	26 Feb	15 Feb	Dragon-dance, antiphonal singing
12 Feb	3 Mar	20 Feb	8 Feb	27 Feb	16 Feb	Lusheng dance, horse race, antiphonal singing
12–14 Feb	3–5 Mar	20–22 Feb	8–10 Feb	27–29 Feb	16–18 Feb	Lusheng dance, bronze drum beating, bullfight
12–14 Feb	4–5 Mar	21–22 Feb	9–10 Feb	28–29 Feb	17–18 Feb	Lusheng dance, bronze drum beating, bullfight
30 Mar	18 Apr	7 Apr	27 Mar	15 Apr	4 Apr	Antiphonal singing, lusheng dance, begging for basket (love)

Festival	Minority Group	No of Partici-pants	Place	Date			
				1994	1995	1996	1997
Sisters' Meal	Miao	30,000	Shidong, Taijiang	25–27 Apr	14–16 Apr	2–4 May	21–23 Apr
Lusheng Festival	Miao	5,000	Taijiang, Huangping, Shibing, Kaili	29 Apr	18–20 Apr	6–8 May	25–27 Apr
Lusheng Festival	Miao	10,000	Xijiang, Leishan	4 May	23 Apr	11 May	30 Apr
Siyueba ('4.8')	Miao	30,000	Guiyang	18 May	7 May	24 May	12 Apr
Siyueba ('4.8')	Miao	15,000	Feiyunyan, Huangping	18 May	7 May	24 May	12 Apr
Junior Dragonboat Festival	Miao	25,000	Shibing	13 Jun	2 Jun	20 Jun	8 Apr
Dragonboat Festival	Miao	30,000	Shidong, Taijiang	5 Jul	24 Jun	12 Jul	1 Jul
Liuyueliu ('6.6')	Bouyei	10,000	Huaxi, Guiyang	14 Jul	3 Jul	21 Jul	8 Aug
Liuyueliu ('6.6')	Miao	3,000	Kaili	14 Jul	3 Jul	21 Jul	8 Aug
New Rice Eating Festival	Miao	3,000	Area bordering Kaili and Taijiang	26 Jul	15 Jul	2 Aug	20 Aug

Date						Activities
1998	1999	2000	2001	2002	2003	
11–13 Apr	30 Apr –2 May	19–21 Apr	8–10 Apr	27–29 Apr	16–18 Apr	Mountain climbing, dating (youfang), dancing to drum, lusheng dance
15–17 May	4–6 May	23–25 Apr	12–14 Apr	1–3 May	20–22 Apr	Lusheng dance, bullfight, horse race
20 Apr	9 May	28 Apr	17 Apr	6 May	25–27 Apr	Bronze drum beating, lusheng dance, begging for embroidered band
2 Apr	21 Apr	10 Apr	30 Mar	18 Apr	7 Apr	Lusheng dance, begging for embroidered band
2 Apr	21 Apr	10 Apr	30 Mar	18 Apr	7 Apr	Lusheng dance, cockfight, horse race
29 May	17 Apr	6 Apr	26 Mar	14 Apr	3 Apr	Dragonboat race, horse race, cockfight
21 Jun	10 Jul	28 Jun	18 Jun	7 Jul	26 Jun	Rowing dragonboat for gifts, dance to drum, horse race
28 Jul	16 Aug	5 Aug	26 Jul	14 Aug	3 Aug	Singing competition
28 Jul	16 Aug	5 Aug	26 Jul	14 Aug	3 Aug	Eating cooked new rice, lusheng dance, bullfight
9 Aug	28 Aug	17 Aug	7 Aug	26 Aug	15 Aug	Lusheng dance, bullfight, antiphonal singing

(clockwise) *Black Miao women welcoming guests, near Xingren; Big Flowery Miao welcoming guests with a dance, near Weining; the silversmith's daughter preparing for a festival, near Shidong*

Miao girls dressing for a lusheng festival, Zhouxi

Small Flowery Miao playing the lusheng pipes, Nankai

Festival	Minority Group	No of Partici-pants	Place	Date			
				1994	1995	1996	1997
Mountain Climbing	Miao	30,000	Xiang Lu Shan (Mt Incense Pot), Kaili	26–28 Jul	16–18 Jul	3–5 Aug	21–23 Aug
Qiyueban ('7.15')	Miao	20,000	Kaili	19 Aug	8 Aug	26 Aug	14 Sept
Lusheng Festival	Miao	10,000	Panghai, Kaili	27 Aug	16 Aug	3 Sept	22 Sept
Chixing Festival (enjoy the happiness of harvest)	Miao	10,000	Xijiang, Leishan	21 Sept	16 Sept	28 Sept	17 Oct
Double Ninth ('9.9')	Miao	5,000	Qingman, Kaili	13 Oct	1 Nov	20 Oct	8 Nov
Miao New Year	Miao	5,000	Guading, Zhouxi, Kaili	6 Nov	25 Nov	14 Nov	3 Dec
Lusheng Festival	Miao	5,000	Xijiang, Leishan	1 Jan	22 Dec	10 Jan	30 Dec

Date						Activities
1998	1999	2000	2001	2002	2003	
10–12 Aug	29–31 Aug	18–20 Aug	8–10 Aug	27–29 Aug	16–18 Aug	Lusheng dance, antiphonal singing, dating (youfang)
3 Sept	22 Sept	10 Sept	31 Aug	19 Sept	9 Sept	Lusheng dance, bullfight, horse race
11 Sept	30 Sept	18 Sept	8 Sept	27 Sept	17 Sept	Lusheng dance, antiphonal singing, horse race
6 Oct	24 Oct	13 Oct	2 Oct	21 Oct	11 Oct	Lusheng dance, antiphonal singing, horse race, bullfight
27 Oct	16 Nov	4 Nov	25 Oct	13 Nov	2 Nov	Lusheng dance, bullfight, horse race
22 Nov	11 Dec	29 Nov	18 Nov	7 Dec	7 Nov	Lusheng dance, bullfight, bronze drum beating
19 Dec	7 Jan	26 Dec	15 Dec	3 Jan	23 Dec	Lusheng dance, bronze drum beating, begging for embroidered band

Practical Information

Hotels

GUIYANG

■ GUIZHOU PARK HOTEL
66 Beijing Road. Tel (0851) 622888,
623888; telex 66075 GZPH CN; fax
(0851) 624397
贵州饭店　北京路66号
Three-star. 31 storey de luxe hotel, 410
twin rooms with bath and shower. Superior rooms available. Eight dining rooms
and banqueting facilities. A good Western breakfast is rarely served. Fair to
good Chinese food, but good Sichuan
and local Guizhou-style banquets can be
organized. Shops, bank, business centre,
bars and dance floor. Staff try to please
and rooms are very comfortable. It is the
best hotel in Guizhou. US$60–100 per
room or suite.

■ GUIYANG PLAZA HOTEL (JINZHU)
2 Yanan Dong Road. Tel (0851) 625888;
telex 66001 PLAZA CN; fax (0851)
622994
贵阳金筑大酒店　延安东路2号
Three-star. Standard twin rooms with
bath and shower. Several restaurants,
shopping arcade, business centre, bank,
bar and karaoke. Excellent central position for shopping. Rooms are comfortable. Restaurants have moderately good
service, poor Western breakfast and good
Chinese food, tending to Cantonese
style. Banquets can be organized. US$65–
85 per room or suite.

■ GUIZHOU HUAXI GUEST HOUSE
Weizai, Huaxi. Tel (0851) 551973,
551129; telex 66017 HXHTL CN
贵州花溪宾馆　花溪围寨
Three-star. A delightful hotel set in the
rolling countryside of Huaxi; very quiet
and restful. There are some superb large
twin rooms with beautiful views. Some
small standard rooms. One small shop.
Many of the political leaders have stayed
here, including Zhou En Lai and Jiang
Zemin. US$50–200 per room or suite.

These three hotels listed above are those
customarily used by foreigners but others
include the following two-star hotels:

■ GUIYANG JIN QIAO HOTEL
36 Ruijinzhong Road. Tel (0851)
517921, 514872
贵阳金桥饭店　瑞金中路36号
About US$25–30 per room.

■ GUIZHOU YUNYAN HOTEL
68 Beijing Road. Tel (0851) 623324
贵州云岩宾馆　北京路68号
Centrally located, but service is not efficient. About US$30 per room.

■ SHENG-AN HOTEL
180–182 Zhongshan East Road.
Tel (0851) 525322; fax 525483
盛安酒店　中山东路180号-182号
Centrally located business hotel. About
US$35 per room.

(preceding pages) *Lush, waterlogged terraced valley and hills*

■ HUALIAN BUILDING
137 Zhong Hua Zhong Lu. Tel (0851) 524298
华联酒店　中华中路137号
Recently opened. US$30–55 per room or suite.

■ TONG DA HOTEL
107 Zunyi Road. Tel (0851) 521910
通达饭店　遵义路107号
Next to the railway station. About US$30 per room.

The following is a budget hostel:

■ DUJUAN HOTEL
17 Yanan Xiang. Tel (0851) 629463, 629465, 624255
杜鹃饭店　延安巷17号
Near the bus station. Popular with backpackers. Dormitory bed US$2, room US$8.

ANSHUN
ANSHUN CITY:
■ ANSHUN MINZU HOTEL
67 Tashan East Road. Tel (0853) 222621; telex 2469
安顺民族饭店　塔山东路67号
A newly renovated hotel with 63 rooms, conveniently located. Muslim and Chinese restaurants. Business centre. About US$30 per room.

■ HONGSHAN HOTEL
73 Baihong Road. Tel (0853) 223101
虹山宾馆　白虹路73号
One wing is being renovated and will be ready in 1995. Set in pretty grounds. About US$30 per room.

■ XI XIU SHAN HOTEL
63 Nanhua Lu. Tel (0853) 224230
西秀山宾馆　南华路63号
The hotel is State-run and not too well looked after. Close to bus and railway stations. About US$10–55 per room.

HUANGGUOSHU WATERFALL AREA:
Huangguoshu, Shibanfang and Tian Xing Lou hotels are under the same management and share phone numbers. Ask for the required hotel extension.

■ HUANGGUOSHU HOTEL
Huangguoshu. Tel (0853) 225243, 223886
黄果树宾馆　黄果树
A new hotel opened in 1992 with 49 pleasant standard rooms, ten of which are air-conditioned. About US$20 per room.

■ SHIBANFANG (STONE HOUSE) HOTEL
Huangguoshu.
石板房　黄果树
A charming older hotel with 16 rooms and good views from the grounds situated close to the waterfall. About US$35–40 per room.

■ TIAN XING LOU HOTEL
Huangguoshu.
天星楼宾馆　黄果树
Chinese-style guesthouse. 24 rooms with private bathrooms, about US$10 per room. Four-bed dormitories without bathrooms, about US$5 per room.

■ **DRAGON PALACE HOTEL**
Ma Tou Xiang, Dragon Palace area
龙宫酒店　马头乡，龙宫
Charming little hotel by the river. 25
rooms, about US$20 per room.

■ **DRAGON PALACE GUEST HOUSE**
Ma Tou Xiang, Dragon Palace area. Tel
(0853) 224950
龙宫宾馆　马头乡，龙宫
Older hotel looking down on the river,
with two wings, one in Chinese-style
architecture, the other new wing in
Western style. The new wing has 64
standard rooms, about US$14 per room.
The old wing offers triple rooms without
bathrooms for about US$4 per room or
standard rooms for about US$35 per
room.

KAILI

■ **YINGPANPO MINZU HOTEL (THE
NATIONAL GUEST HOUSE)**
53 East Yingpanpo Road. Tel (0855)
223163
营盘坡民族宾馆　营盘坡东路53号
There are two main buildings of standard
rooms with bath and WC. Even the
newer wing is run down and the water
and electricity often fail. However, beds
are comfortable and clean and guests are
welcomed by girls in ethnic costume.
The attached restaurant has mediocre
food. There is an excellent shop that sells
ethnic costume. Prices are relatively high.
Outside the hotel peasants gather to sell
costume and embroidery and there are
two shops opposite the hotel gates that
sell costume. Bargaining recommended.
US$10–20 per room.

■ **HONG ZHOU HOTEL**
55 Hong Zhou Lu. Tel (0855) 2256801,
223689
红洲饭店　红洲路55号
44 standard rooms with private bathrooms. About US$15–20 per room.

■ **KAILI HOTEL**
3 Guangchang Lu. Tel (0855) 224466
凯里宾馆　广场路3号
52 standard rooms with private bathrooms. About US$25–30 per room.

■ **ZI ZHU YUAN HOTEL**
92 Huancheng Road West. Tel (0855)
221875
紫竹苑饭店　广场西路92号
23 standard rooms with private bathrooms. About US$16 per room.

XIJIANG

■ **XIJIANG RECEPTION HOUSE
(ZHAODAISUO)**
Xijiang.
西江招待所　西江
Basic rooms with communal washing
facilities and toilets.

TAIJIANG, ZHENYUAN, SHIDONG, RONGJIANG, CONGJIANG, ZHAOXING, LIPING

Chinese-style guest houses, generally
without private facilities, offer twin-
bedded rooms with hard mattress and
warm duvet at these towns. Dormitory
rooms are also available. Mosquito nets
are provided. Communal washplaces and
toilets. Toilets flush irregularly and are
sometimes not very clean. At Zhaoxing
there is a small new wooden hotel that is

Rape flowers in bloom in February, Qingzhen area

tastefully designed in the Dong style and worth a visit.

TONGREN
■ JINJIANG HOTEL
Jinjiang Road. Tel (0856) 23093, 23094
锦江宾馆　锦江路
Standard hotel of twin-bedded rooms with bath and WC. Excellent restaurant attached to the hotel; banquets are beautifully served. About US$10–20 per room.

ZUNYI
■ ZUNYI HOTEL
Zhiyi Road, old part of Zunyi City. Tel (0852) 223142
遵义宾馆　遵义老城
There is only one modern wing with 11 rooms but the hotel has the advantage of being situated near the river with good views of Phoenix Mountain, site of the Red Army monument. About US$10–40 per room.

■ XIANGSHAN HOTEL
Wanli Road. Tel (0852) 225754
香山饭店　万里路
Standard rooms with bath and WC, some with air conditioning. This is considered the best hotel in Zunyi. About US$30 per room.

LIUPANSHUI (LIUZHI, SHUICHENG, PAN XIAN) LIUZHI:
■ THE SECOND ZHAODAISUO OF THE PEOPLE'S GOVERNMENT
Friendship Road. Tel (08681) 22660
第二人民政府招待所　友谊路
Very pleasant rooms; some have small private bathrooms. A good view. About US$5–15 per room.

■ LIUZHI HOTEL
Tuanjie Road. Tel (08681) 22367
六枝饭店　团结路
This hotel belongs to the Mining Bureau
and has standard rooms with antiquated
facilities. There are some rooms with en
suite living rooms. Old fashioned decor.
About US$10–20 per room.

SHUICHENG:

■ ZHONGSHAN HOTEL
52 Zhongshan West Road. Tel (0858)
223863
中山饭店　中山西路52号
One floor has been newly refurbished
with bathroom facilities but WC is still
unreliable. Hot water is intermittent.
Rooms fairly clean. New restaurant, fair
food. About US$10–20 per room.

PAN XIAN:

■ PAN XIAN RECEPTION HOUSE
　(ZHAODAISUO)
Pan Xian. Tel (08682) 22217
盘县招待所　盘县
Of the 40 rooms only 5 or 6 have private
bathrooms. Excellent food and a pretty
garden. About US$5–15 per room.

DUYUN

■ DRAGON POOL HOTEL (LONG TAN)
276 Huangdong Zhong Road. Tel (0854)
222269; telex 0146
龙潭宾馆　环车中路276号
170 standard twin rooms; many with
bath and WC. The hotel is on the river
and some rooms have good views of
Wenfeng Pagoda. The rooms are fairly
well cared for and there has been an
attempt at modernization in some rooms.

Hot water is intermittent. There are
several large restaurants. In 1993, the
Foreign Affairs Office initiated a Tea
Ceremony at the hotel. This can be
booked through the hotel or Foreign
Affairs Office. Several teas are served in a
variety of local ways interspersed with
food, all of which is traditional to the
area. Young girls show how the tea is
prepared on an attractive stage set. Ex-
planations are given in different languages and it makes an interesting
evening. About US$15–30 per room.

■ HONG KONG HOTEL
(formerly Yunchen Hotel)
134 Hebin Road. Tel (0854) 222896
香港宾馆　河滨路134号
About US$10–25 per room.

XINGYI

■ PANJIANG HOTEL
Panjiangxi Road. Tel (0859) 223524
盘江宾馆　盘江西路
About US$6–22 per room.

ZHENFENG

■ ZHENFENG RECEPTION HOUSE
　(ZHAODAISUO)
Zhenfeng.
贞丰招待所　贞丰
Basic rooms. Communal washing facili-
ties and toilets. Hot water supplied.
About US$5–10 per room.

WEINING

■ WEINING RECEPTION HOUSE
　(ZHAODAISUO)
Weining. Tel 22496. No direct dial.

Please call operator for assistance.
威宁招待所　威宁
Some twin rooms with private bathrooms and dormitories. Some rooms have been whitewashed and new beds and TV fitted. Hot water is intermittent and rooms may be dusty. About US$5–12 per room.

BIJIE
■ HONGSHAN HOTEL
5 Hongshan Road. Tel (0857) 23891
洪山饭店　洪山路 5 号
Standard rooms with private bathrooms, but not very well cared for. About US$20 per room.

Restaurants

With the new free-market economy, restaurants are opening and closing all the time. Some become fashionable for a while, lose their popularity and deteriorate, or do not make a profit and close. Ask advice from the local people about where to eat.

GUIYANG
■ OVERSEAS FRIENDSHIP RESTAURANT
4 Yanan East Road. Tel (0851) 622768
海外友谊酒家　延安东路 4 号
Good local food.

■ YAYUAN RESTAURANT
33 Beijing Road. Tel (0851) 624111
雅园酒家　北京路33号
Good local food.

■ JUE YUAN VEGETARIAN RESTAURANT
51 Fu Shui Road North. Tel (0851) 529609
觉园素餐馆　富水北路57号
Run by nuns.

■ HONGFU TEMPLE VEGETARIAN RESTAURANT
Hongfu Temple, Qianling Park. Tel (0851) 625606
弘福寺素餐馆　黔灵公园弘福寺
Run by monks.

KAILI
■ YAYUAN RESTAURANT
Xincheng Road South. Tel (0855) 223002
雅园饭店　新城南路

■ MOONLIGHT RESTAURANT
2 Shaoshan Road South. Tel (0855) 225561
月光饭店　韶山南路 2 号

■ KUAIHUOLIN RESTAURANT
West end of Kaili city on the road to Guiyang.
快活林饭店　凯里城西端
Specializing in Miao-style spicy fish soup (*suan tang yu*).

TONGREN
■ MILKY WAY GRAND RESTAURANT
Gongqing Road. Tel (0856) 23296
银路大饭店　恭请路

ZUNYI
■ GOOD FRIEND RESTAURANT
Yanan Road. Tel (0852) 225428
好友饭店　延安路

■ THE 90S MUSIC RESTAURANT
90 Zhongshan Road. Tel (0852) 222685
九十年代音乐饭店　中山路90号

LIUPANSHUI (LIUZHI,
SHUICHENG, PAN XIAN)
LIUZHI:
■ CHAO YANG BUILDING RESTAURANT
Tuanjie Road. Tel (08681) 22623
朝阳饭店　团结路

■ SOUTH CHINA RESTAURANT
Nanping Road. Tel (08681) 22520
中国南方饭店　南平路

SHUICHENG:
■ MINZU RESTAURANT
Tel (0858) 224153
民族饭店

DUYUN
■ DUYUN MUSLIM RESTAURANT
Jianjiang Zhong Road. Tel (0854)
223467
都匀清真饭店　剑江中路

■ APRICOT BLOSSOM RESTAURANT
Hebin Road. Tel (0854) 224496
杏花饭店　河滨路

Useful Addresses

GUIYANG
■ GUIYANG RAILWAY STATION
Zunyi Road. Tel (0851) 523762
贵阳火车站　遵义路

■ GUIYANG BUS STATION
Yanan West Road. Tel (0851) 624224
贵阳汽车站　延安西路

■ GUIYANG OVERSEAS CHINESE
FRIENDSHIP COMPANY
4 Yanan East Road. Tel (0851) 626456
贵阳华侨友谊公司　延安东路4号
Large department store.

■ GUIYANG MINZU (NATIONALITIES)
DEPARTMENT STORE
On the southwest of Penshuichi.
贵阳民族商店　喷水池西南面

■ GUIYANG ANTIQUE STORE
9 Gongyuan Road. Tel (0851) 524109
贵阳文物商店　公园路9号

■ GUIYANG XINHUA BOOKSTORE
Zhonghuazhong Road. Tel (0851)
524148
贵阳新华书店　中华中路

■ GUIZHOU MUSEUM
Beijing Road. Tel (0851) 625674
贵州博物馆　北京路

■ GUIZHOU BOTANICAL GARDENS
Liuchongguan. Tel (0851) 622403,
62311
贵阳植物园　六冲关

ANSHUN
■ ANSHUN FOLK CRAFT FACTORY
Xijao, Anshun. Tel (0853) 22796
安顺民族工艺厂　安顺西邮

This covered bridge near Rongjiang, known as a 'wind and rain' bridge, where travellers can take shelter from the elements, is a major feature of Dong architecture

■ THE ANSHUN GENERAL BATIK
   FACTORY
46 Nanhua Road, Anshun. Tel (0853)
22651, 22884, 24420
中国贵州蜡染对外贸易总公司
（安顺蜡染总厂）南华路46号

TAIJIANG
■ MIAO NATIONALITY EMBROIDERY
   AND CRAFT WORKSHOP
444 Heping Street. Tel (08689) 22037
台江苗族刺绣厂　和平路444号
Part of a UNICEF project. Embroideries
and gift items can be bought here. (Director: Yang Hua)

ZUNYI
■ FOREIGN AFFAIRS OFFICE
Zhongshan Road. Tel (0852) 224733
遵义外事办　中山路

■ ZUNYI BUS STATION
Beijing Road.
遵义汽车站　北京路

■ ZUNYI RAILWAY STATION
Beijing Road. Tel (0852) 22213, 22235
遵义火车站　北京路

LIUPANSHUI (LIUZHI, SHUICHENG, PAN XIAN)
■ FOREIGN AFFAIRS OFFICE
Room 336, Zhongshan Hotel, Shuicheng.
Tel (0858) 222597, 223663
六盘水外事办　水城中山宾馆336房间

DUYUN
■ FOREIGN AFFAIRS OFFICE
Dragon Pool Hotel, 276 Huangdong
Zhong Road. Tel (0854) 221211
黔南州外事办　环车中路276号龙潭宾馆内

BIJIE

■ **BIJIE BUS STATION**
Weixi Road.
毕节汽车站　威西路

Markets

GUIYANG

■ **LIXIN ROAD AGRICULTURAL PRODUCE MARKET**
Situated along Lixin Road and Heping Road.
立新路农贸市场　立新路和平路
One of the largest free markets selling vegetables, fruits, meat, fish and other local delicacies.

■ **CHENGJI ROAD FREE MARKET**
From Weiqingmen to Yanan Street
城基路自由市场　从威清门到延安街
Fresh produce market.

■ **NIGHT MARKETS**
The night markets open at dusk. The biggest include Guanzhuqiao, Xiaoshizi, Dananmen, Longjing Road and Putuo Road. Here you can buy a vast range of delicious meals and snacks, many of which are traditional to the province.

KAILI

■ **SUNDAY MARKET**
Along Yingpanpo Road, a few minutes walk from Yingpanpo Hotel.
星期日集市　营盘坡路
This, the largest market in Kaili is well worth a visit for its local handicrafts, such as embroidery, bird cages, pottery, bamboo baskets and silver jewellery. The best time to visit is between 12:00 and 15:00.

TAIJIANG

■ **TAIJIANG MARKET**
台江集场
Similar to Kaili Market. Look out for indigo, hand-woven fabrics and silver jewellery. The market operates on a five-day cycle.

WEINING

■ **WEINING MARKET**
威宁集市
There is an excellent produce market in the town every four or five days where Yi, Hui and Miao people sell their goods.

Travel Agents and Tour Operators

GUIZHOU
GUIYANG:

■ **GUIZHOU OVERSEAS TRAVEL CORPORATION (GZOTC)**
21 Yanan Zhong Road, Guiyang, 550001.
Tel (0851) 525328, 523433; fax (0851) 523095
贵州海外旅游总公司　贵阳延安中路21号
The Guizhou Overseas Travel Corporation (GZOTC) and the Guizhou Everbright Travel Incorporation (GZETI) are both under the Guizhou Provincial Tourism Administration. This is the largest travel corporation in the province and has agencies in over 30 countries and regions around the world, including the

US, Japan and Hong Kong, with well-trained guides who speak English, French, German, Japanese, Thai and Korean. Many of the guides have over ten years experience in the travel industry. Long-term contracts with CAAC, for which it is a booking agent covering domestic and international flights, the railway stations and the hotels ensure a comprehensive and efficient service to tourists and travellers in the province. Special services on offer include scenic, ethnic culture, hiking, motorcycle and jeep tours. The corporation also arranges tours for Guizhou citizens to Southeast Asia, Hong Kong, Macau and Taiwan.

■ CHINA INTERNATIONAL TRAVEL SERVICE, GUIYANG BRANCH
11 Yanan Zhong Road, Guiyang, 550001. Tel (0851) 525873; fax (0851) 524222
贵州中国国际旅行社　延安中路11号

■ CIVIL AVIATION ADMINISTRATION OF CHINA (CAAC)
264 Zunyi Road. Tel (0851) 523000
中国民航　遵义路264号

■ GUIZHOU INTERNATIONAL TRAVEL AIR SERVICE COMPANY
Guiyang Plaza Hotel. Tel (0851) 625888 extension 1507
贵州国际航空服务部　金筑酒店

ANSHUN:
■ ANSHUN TRAVEL SERVICE
City Hall, G/F, 2 Tashan Road West, Anshun. Tel (0853) 223224, 224815
安顺旅行社　塔山西路 2 号
　　　　　市政府大楼内 1 楼

■ ANSHUN MINZU TRAVEL SERVICE
Minzu Hotel. Tel (0853) 222621; telex 2469
安顺民族旅行社　民族饭店

KAILI:
■ CHINA INTERNATIONAL TRAVEL SERVICE, KAILI BRANCH
53 East Yingpanpo Road (in the entrance of the Yingpanpo Minzu Hotel). Tel (0855) 222506; fax (0855) 222547
中国国际旅行社　凯里支社　营盘坡东路53号
　　　　　　　　　　　　营盘坡民族宾馆内

TONGREN:
■ TONGREN TRAVEL SERVICE
117 Zhongshan Road. Tel (0856) 23764
铜仁旅行社　中山路117号

ZUNYI:
■ ZUNYI TRAVEL SERVICE
109 Xiangshan Hotel. Tel (0852) 224991 extension 109, 424
遵义旅行社　香山宾馆109号

XINGYI:
■ TOURISM BUREAU OF XINGYI CITY
City Government Courtyard. Tel (0859) 223492
兴义旅游局　政府大院

HONG KONG
■ CHINA STAR TRAVEL LIMITED, GUIZHOU OVERSEAS TRAVEL CORPORATION, HONG KONG BRANCH
1308 Wayson Commercial Building, 28 Connaught Road West, Hong Kong. Tel (852) 5461613, 5461846; fax (852) 5590648
中国之星旅行社有限公司　贵州海外旅游总公司驻
　　　　　　　　　　　香港总代理
　　　　　　　　　　　香港干诺道西28号
　　　　　　　　　　　威胜商业大厦1308室

■ **CHINA NATIONAL AVIATION CORPO-RATION**
Ticketing Office, 17 Queens Road, Central, Hong Kong. Reservations tel (852) 8610322; fax (852) 5285181
中国航空公司　中环皇后大道中17号

■ **CHINA TRAVEL SERVICE (HK) LIMITED**
Foreign Passenger Department, 4/F, CTS House, 78–83 Connaught Road, Central, Hong Kong. Tel 8533888; fax (852) 5419777
香港中国旅行社　干诺道中78-83号
中旅集团大厦 4 楼

UNITED KINGDOM
■ **OCCIDOR ADVENTURE TOURS LIMITED**
10 Broomcroft Road, Bognor Regis, West Sussex, PO22 7NJ. Tel (0243) 582178; fax (0243) 587239

■ **AIR CHINA**
41 Grosvenor Gardens, London, SW1W 0BP. Tel (071) 6300919, 6307678; fax (071) 6307792

UNITED STATES OF AMERICA
■ **FAR VILLAGE**
310 Beloit Avenue, Los Angeles, Ca 90049. Tel (310) 472 8734; fax (310) 4765997

(above) *An overview of modern Guiyang*
(opposite page) *An old bridge with modern pavilion, Zhenyuan*

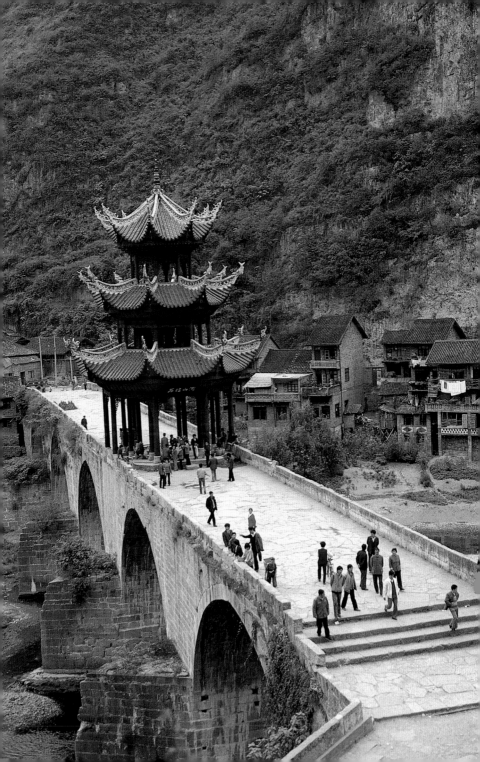

Turn of the century photograph of a Miao woman weaving on a backstrap loom

A Guide to Pronouncing Chinese Names

The official system of Romanization used in China, which the visitor will find on maps, road signs and city shopfronts, is known as *Pinyin*. It is now almost universally adopted by the Western media.

Some visitors may initially encounter some difficulty in pronouncing Romanized Chinese words. In fact many of the sounds correspond to the usual pronunciation of the letters in English. The exceptions are:

Initials

c	is like the *ts* in 'it*s*'
q	is like the *ch* in 'cheese'
x	has no English equivalent, and can best be described as a hissing consonant that lies somewhere between *sh* and *s*. The sound was rendered as *hs* under an earlier transcription system.
z	is like the *ds* in 'fa*ds*'
zh	is unaspirated, and sounds like the *j* in 'jug'.

Finals

a	sounds like 'ah'
e	is pronounced as in 'her'
i	is pronounced as in 'ski' (written as *yi* when not preceded by an initial consonant). However, in *ci, chi, ri, shi, zi* and *zhi*, the sound represented by the final is quite different and is similar to the *ir* in 'sir' but without much stressing of the *r* sound.
o	sounds like the *aw* in 'law'
u	sounds like the *oo* in 'ooze'
ü	is pronounced as the German *ü* (written as *yu* when not preceded by an initial consonant). The *ê* and *ü* are usually written simply as *e* and *u*.

Finals in Combination

When two or more finals are combined, such as in *hao, jiao* and *liu*, each letter retains its sound value as indicated in the list above, but note the following:

ai   is like the *ie* in 'tie'
ei   is like the *ay* in 'bay'
ian   is like the *ien* in 'Vienna'
ie   similar to 'ear'
ou   is like the *o* in 'code'
uai   sounds like 'why'
uan   is like the *uan* in 'iguana'
            (except when proceeded by *j, q, x* and *y*; in these cases a *u*
            following any of these four consonants is in fact *ü* and *uan* is
            similar to *uen*.)
ue   is like the *ue* in 'duet'
ui   sounds like 'way'

Examples

A few Chinese names are shown below with English phonetic spelling beside
them:

Beijing	Bay-jing
Cixi	Tsi-shee
Guilin	Gway-lin
Hangzhou	Hahng-joe
Kangxi	Kahng-shee
Qianlong	Chien-loong
Tiantai	Tien-tie
Xian	Shee-ahn

An apostrophe is used to separate syllables in certain compound-character
words to preclude confusion. For example, *Changan* (which can be *chang-an*
or *chan-gan*) is sometimes written as *Chang'an*.

Tones

A Chinese syllable consists of not only an initial and a final or finals, but also
a tone or pitch of the voice when the words are spoken. In *Pinyin* the four
basic tones are marked ‾ , ´ , ˇ and ` . These marks are almost never shown in
printed form except in language texts.

A Chronology of Chinese Dynasties

Hsia	21st–16th century BC
Shang	16th–11th century BC
Western Zhou	11th century–771 BC
Spring and Autumn Period	770–476 BC
Warring States Period	475–221 BC
Qin	221–206 BC
Western Han	206 BC–AD 24
Eastern Han	25–220
Three Kingdoms	220–265
Western Jin	265–316
Eastern Jin	317–420
Southern and Northern Dynasties	420–581
Sui	581–618
Tang	618–907
Five Dynasties	907–960
Song	960–1279
Jin	1115–1234
Yuan	1279–1368
Ming	1368–1644
Qing	1644–1911
Republic of China	1911–1949
People's Republic of China	1949–

Wuyang River and Gorge

Recommended Reading

Travel Guides and Tourism

Stevens, K Mark and Wehrfritz, G E, *Southwest China: Off The Beaten Track* (Collins, London, 1988)

Xu Lang et al, *Guiyang* (New World Press, Beijing, 1989)

'Guizhou Special', *China Tourism*, no 104 (Hong Kong Tourism Press, Hong Kong, Feb 1989)

'Guizhou's National Festivals', booklet produced by the Foreign Affairs office of the Guizhou Provincial Peoples' Government (Guizhou Arts Publishing House, 1987)

'Guizhou—A Treasure to be explored', booklet produced by the Guizhou Advertising Company (Guiyang)

Ethnic Groups and Textiles

Cooper, Robert et al, *The Hmong* (Artasia Press Co Ltd, Bangkok, 1991)

Cultural Palace of Nationalities, Beijing (ed), *Clothings and Ornaments of China's Miao People* (The Nationality Press, Beijing, 1985)

Gösta Sandberg, *Indigo Textiles: Technique and History* (A & C Black, London, 1989)

Huang Shoubao, *Ethnic Costume from Guizhou* (Foreign Languages Press, Beijing, 1987)

Lam Ping-fai, Robert (ed), *Ethnic Costumes of the Miao People in China* (Urban Council, Hong Kong, 1985)

Laumann, Maryta (ed), *Miao Textile Design* (Fu Jen Catholic University Press, Taipei, 1993)

Lu Pu, *Designs of Chinese Indigo Batik* (New World Press, Beijing, 1981)

Mallinson, Jane; Donnelly, Nancy and Ly Hang, *H'mong Batik: A Textile Technique from Laos* (Mallinson Information Services, Seattle, 1988)

Ma Yin (ed), *China's Minority Nationalities* (Foreign Languages Press, Beijing, 1989)

Rossi, Gail, 'Growing Indigo', *Surface Design Journal* (Surface Design Association, Oakland, California, Summer 1988)

Rossi, Gail, *The Dong People of China* (Hagley & Hoyle, Singapore, 1990)

Shi Songshan (chief editor), *The Costumes and Adornments of Chinese Yi Nationality Picture Album* (Beijing Art & Crafts Publishing House, Beijing, 1989)

Wei Ronghui (ed), *The Chinese National Culture of Costume and Adornment* (China Textile Press, Beijing)

Zeng Xianyang, *The Happy People-The Miaos* (Foreign Languages Press, Beijing, 1988)

Richly Woven Traditions: Costumes of the Miao of Southwest China and Beyond, catalogue produced by the China Institute in America (China House Gallery, New York, 1988)

Hmong Art: Tradition and Change, catalogue produced by the John Michael Kohler Arts Center (Sheboygan, Wisconsin, 1985)

Literature and History

Bosshardt, Alfred and England, G and E, *The Guiding Hand* (Hodder & Stoughton, London, 1973)

Bosshardt, R A, *The Restraining Hand* (Hodder & Stoughton, London, first printed 1936)

Broomhall, A J, *Strong Tower* (China Inland Mission, London, 1947)

Broomhall, A J, *Strong Man's Prey* (China Inland Mission, London, 1953)

Clarke, Samuel R, *Among the Tribes in Southwest China* (China Inland Mission, London, 1911)

Foreign Languages Press (ed and translation), *Mao Tse Tung Poems* (Foreign Languages Press, Beijing, 1976)

Geil, William Edgar, *Eighteen Capitals of China* (Constable and Co, London, 1911)

Grey, Anthony, *Peking: A novel of China's Revolution 1921–1978* (Pan Books, London, 1989)

Grist, Reverend W A, *Samuel Pollard, Pioneer Missionary in China* (First published by Cassell, no date, reprinted Ch'eng Wen Publishing Co, Taipei, 1971)

Kemp, E G, *Chinese Mettle*, (Hodder & Stoughton, London, no date)

Kendall, R Elliott, *Beyond the Clouds: The Story of Samuel Pollard* (Cargate Press, London, 1947)

Kendall, R Elliott (ed), *Eyes of the Earth: The Diary of Samuel Pollard* (Cargate Press, London, 1954)

Lin Yueh Hwa, 'The Miao-Man Peoples of Kweichow', *Harvard Journal of Asiatic Studies*, Vol 5, part 2, pp 261–345 (June 1940)

Lindesay, William, Marching with Mao (Hodder & Stoughton, London, 1993)

Mickey, Margaret P, 'The Cowrie Shell Miao of Kweichow', *Papers of the Peabody Museum of American Archaeology and Ethnology*, Vol 32, pp 1–80 (Harvard University, Cambridge, 1947)

Pruen, Mrs, *The Provinces of Western China* (China Inland Mission, London, 1906)
Salisbury, Harrison E, *The Long March: The Untold Story* (Macmillan, London, 1985)
Theroux, Paul, *Riding The Iron Rooster* (Hamish Hamilton, London, 1988)

Flora and Fauna

Lancaster, Roy, *Travels in China—A Plantsman's Paradise* (Antique Collectors' Club, Woodbridge, Suffolk, 1989)
Tang Xiyang, Living Treasures: *An Odyssey through China's Extraordinary Nature Reserves* (Bantam Books, New York, 1987 and New World Press, Beijing, 1987)
Wilson, E H, *A Naturalist in Western China* (Cadogan Books, London, 1986)

Geography

Bucks, J L, *Land Utilisation in China* (University of Nanking, 1937)
Cannon, T and Jenkins, A (eds), *The Geography of Contemporary China* (Routledge, London, 1990)
Tregear, T R, China, *A Geographical Survey* (Hodder & Stoughton, London, 1980)
Atlas of the People's Republic of China (Foreign Language Press, Beijing, 1989)
Southern China, Nelles Verlag Maps, China 4 (Freytag and Berndt, Austria)

Tonggu painting in the primitive style

Index